STAMBOUL GHOSTS

STAMBOUL GHOSTS

A Stroll Through Bohemian Istanbul

JOHN FREELY

Tribute by Andrew Finkel
Afterword by Maureen Freely

PHOTOGRAPHS BY ARA GÜLER

CORNUCOPIA

Contents

*John Freely's First Communion in Brooklyn,
New York City, 1933*

John Freely, 1926–2017
A Tribute by Andrew Finkel

If it was Harry Truman who famously decided that 'the buck stops here', then we had John Freely – physicist, historian, traveller, author and joyful companion – to remind us that the buck had to start somewhere and that he had it on the best authority (and thereby hung an engaging but not-so-simple tale) where that somewhere was. John's novelist daughter Maureen once confessed to the frustration of trying to begin a story set in Istanbul, a city where not even the past stands still. The place you thought you should start was never the place you actually started – and then umpteen drafts later you found yourself starting from somewhere different again. Of course, the easier solution would have been to ask John.

For my generation it was John Freely – not the Milestone by the Hippodrome – that stood at the epicentre of Istanbul. *Strolling Through Istanbul*, the 1972 guidebook that he co-authored with his fellow Robert College professor Hilary Sumner-Boyd, described exactly where to begin the adventure. Page one, chapter one plonks us on the Galata Bridge, facing the Golden Horn and the historic skyline. At a glance we appreciated the intimacy that the city has with the sea and how topography and geography shaped Istanbul's character.

And as we made our way through the museums and the monuments and got lost in the backstreets, John Freely was beside us, with one anecdote after another, chatting, holding our hand.

Better still, he was nudging us in the ribs, telling us when to look up, or round the next corner, or simply to sit down for a moment's reflection.

Bookseller Hugh Grant advises Julia Roberts in the film *Notting Hill* to start with another Freely opus, *Istanbul: The Imperial City*, as one of the few travel books where the author had actually been to the place he describes. Of course, to say that John had set foot in Istanbul was a bit like saying James Joyce had been to Dublin or Damon Runyon to New York. He was no casual visitor but helped define how we perceive the city – almost as much a part of the skyline as the domes and minarets whose geometry he understood so well.

John gave us courage to explore on our own. Book in hand, I knew to hunt for the man with the key to gain entrance to the ruins of St John in Stoudios. Without his advice I might never have stood long and appreciatively before the Anastasis fresco, where a dynamic Jesus physically resurrects the dead in St Saviour in Chora. John spotted the piece of Krupp artillery in the basilica of Aya Irini while it was still a military museum. In the years that followed I would casually, with the air of the young know-it-all I was, point it out

to visiting friends on our way back from Topkapı Palace.

Strolling's entry on Saints Sergius and Bacchus, by its very length and wealth of detail, helped restore the dignity of such an important but at the time much-ignored monument. It included a floor plan of the church-turned-mosque, built along a squiffy axis. But this was no dry Baedeker description. 'As in almost all of the surviving Byzantine churches of the city, we must simply use our imagination in order to recapture the extraordinary beauty of its original condition,' he wrote in his ceaseless endeavour to make us see past the façade of the present – advice badly ignored in the building's recent careless over-restoration.

John had a matchmaker's skill in making us feel – improbable as it seems in what has become the most populous city in Europe – that we had Istanbul and its history all to ourselves. It was more than forty years ago, but I remember the excitement in his voice, one summer, when he told me that the sultan's lodge in the New Mosque (Yeni Cami) had just been opened to the public to display a collection of carpets. I followed his instructions to the door at a concealed higher level at the back of the mosque

John, aged 17, on enlisting in the US Navy, and Dolores, after the war, aged 18

– the private royal entrance. A few months later, I tried to go again but the door was chained and, as far as I know, has remained locked ever since. The New Mosque overlooks a busy commuting hub, crowded by day and mostly by night. There are still times when I smile to think that I know one of its secrets.

John's own guide was the seventeenth-century traveller Evliya Çelebi – an itinerant courtier who travelled the Empire and never took the shortest route when a circuitous one would do. Evliya's *Britannica*-thick account of his travels, what he saw, whom he spoke to, all peppered by a liberal imagination, captured the spirit of place after place. John discovered an ancient translation of the Istanbul section of Evliya's *Seyyahatname* in the college library during the very first week after he arrived, and was inspired to adopt the same narrative style. Evliya's observations are cited with great frequency in *Strolling* and Evliya is the acknowledged muse of John's own lyrical daybook, *Stamboul Sketches*.

Like Evliya, John was happiest on the road. He wrote about so many places and so many things: biographies, guides, compendia on subjects as disparate as the Seljuk dynasty and the history of science. He could produce another volume in the time it took others to clear their throats. Those who delighted in his company could also bristle about his intrusion into their own discipline. It is, however, a tautology born of envy to call a man who produced sixty-five books a generalist. It is true he would sometimes raid past work to produce the next. But even scholars have to live, and who isn't guilty of telling a good story twice?

How John survived could not entirely be explained by the laws of physics that he taught. Family and friends sat down last May in Istanbul to his funeral feast at Asmalı Cavit, a Beyoğlu meyhane that John loved. When it was time to leave, the eponymous proprietor Cavit Saatçi would not accept a penny – a generous gesture for sure, but a fitting tribute to a man who lived off the devotion he inspired. The spiritual guru Krishnamurti reportedly travelled

The Freelys aboard the 'Marmara', sailing from Istanbul to Antalya, January 1961

the world without a penny in his pocket, supported and cosseted by a committed following. And while there was something about John being able to float through air, there were times when I thought of him affectionately as one of my favourite characters in SJ Perelman's humorous pieces for *The New Yorker* – the chap in the Dublin pub who, with an innocent air, gets by selling literary anecdotes about Leopold Bloom to passing American academics.

To declare my own interest, I first met John in 1968, when I was barely a teenager, as the parent of my friends. My first recollection (though it may be a fictive memory) is of a conversation at a rickety table at Nazmi's, the famous garden meyhane on the shore in Küçük Bebek, where much of the real education of Robert College took place. It is not correct to say that John held court. He came to converse. The pleasure I recall (apart from being able at that young age to cadge one of those high-necked brown bottles of state-monopoly beer) is that he did not speak as professor to schoolboy but assumed an equality.

It is that openness, I surmise, his public lack of guile, which made him a memorable teacher and beloved colleague. I grew accustomed over the years to seeing the faces of his former

students light up on learning that John was back to teaching at what had become Bosphorus University. On reflection, it is also the quality that makes his books a delight. He wrote not as an expert but as a friend eager to share. Of course, he had read around his subject, found the apposite, erudite quote, walked miles by day and burned the oil at his writing desk into the night. He had a rare affinity to engage instantly with what he saw and whom he met. But his body language was that he was merely doing something anyone could.

Almost anyone. His extraordinary moment, the one that lay at the heart of his final autobiographical books, was the bungee-jumping-off-the-Brooklyn-Bridge lack of caution that in 1960 pushed him to abandon a research position in Princeton in search of adventure. He took a job at Robert College, a liberal arts college on the Bosphorus, whose existence he had learned of by happenstance after falling into conversation with a faculty member. He had made a pact with his wife, Dolores, to lead a life of travel, and by his own account (*The Art of Exile: A Vagabond Life* was published in 2016) it took no persuasion to convince her to pack up the three children, aged between one and eight, and board a plane for Istanbul.

I read recently an account by the journalist Suzy Hansen of unravelling her own not quite rational decision to leave New York. The pin Hansen stuck in the map also landed in Istanbul, largely because she was curious to know how the author James Baldwin could have felt freer there as a gay black man than he had in Paris or New York. Would Baldwin have felt quite so liberated if he had not been a frequent guest at John Freely's parties and experienced that Never-Never-Land sense of bohemia among the expatriate faculty in an outrageously beautiful campus overlooking the Straits? I have heard from more than one source the tale of John's joyful, inebriated chorus of 'Smoke Gets in Your Eyes' as the firemen arrived at his university lodgings to put out a blaze in the flue of the wood-burning stove.

Baldwin left Shangri-La, drawn back to his own New York reality. John, too, made sojourns elsewhere (*Strolling Through Athens* appeared in 1991, *Strolling Through Venice* in 1994). But he returned to Istanbul. It is odd, I suppose, that he was adopted by a country whose language he never really knew. His reality was not the Istanbul of the here and now

John Freely with his daughter Maureen Freely on the Bosphorus campus of Robert College in 2001

but uncovering layer after layer, deciphering palimpsest upon palimpsest in the city he had made his own.

In *Stamboul Ghosts*, he tells of his first meeting with Baldwin at one of the famous Robert College parties. 'He had been a shoeshine boy and worked in a sweatshop, whereas I had been a scavenger and worked in a condom factory. Jimmy had left the US and made a new life in France, just as Toots

[John's name for Dolores] and I were doing in Turkey.' John was simply a member of a different underclass.

The House of Memory: Reflections on Youth and War, published in 2018, is remarkable first as a crystal-clear recollection of a nonagenarian's early years, but also for the story it tells of a childhood spent shuttling between his mother's birthplace in County Kerry and his native Brooklyn while his father looked for work. John dropped out of high school, joined the Navy and took part in the brutal Burma campaign. This allowed him to

PANDORA LONGSTRETH

John with granddaughters Pandora and Helen in 2015 on his last visit to the family home in Dingle, County Kerry

ride the GI Bill into university and from there to obtain a doctorate at NYU. There is a huge difference between enjoying the privilege of good fortune and having a privileged sense of entitlement.

John was not ignorant of change but he knew how to make it behave and put a higher value on the things that remain.

That the ghosts of this current volume lived in 'Stamboul' (not, as the song would have it, Istanbul or Constantinople) denotes a certain wistfulness. Though published posthumously, it is still hard to believe there is not one more book up his sleeve. And if we turn page after page, it is precisely because we feel we are at the end of an evening and reluctant to go home, so we stay for just one more story, and one more after that. Here, he writes not just *as* a friend, but *about* his friends, and he does so with affection and irreverence and in a way that, in more than one place, is laugh-out-loud funny. Some of the cast of characters I knew, and I can report that, while they may seem Runyonesque, they are Freelyesque glimpses into the frailties that make people real. I myself make a discreet cameo – in case you were wondering who, in the photo of John and Toots

Good times rolling: John Freely in the back of a vintage Cadillac with his wife, Toots, in sunglasses and the Byzantinist Bob Ousterhout raising his hat. The photo was taken in 2011 by another old Istanbul friend, Tony Greenwood

riding in the back of a vintage Cadillac, was riding in the front passenger seat, his face entirely eclipsed by the driver.

In the chapter on *Strolling*, John writes how he still hears the voice of his co-author Hilary Sumner-Boyd in phrases that survived the many revisions – speaking, cocktail in hand, from beyond the grave. But it is unmistakably John's voice we hear in *Strolling Through Istanbul*'s final chapter – itself called, not surprisingly, 'The Last Stroll'. It was written by a man halfway though his life and much too young to be his own epitaph:

'The old town, for all its faults and flaws, has managed to retain some of the humane qualities of communal life and rich connections with the past that

have been lost in most modern cities. In that mood we think of our own strolls through Stamboul and of the dear friends who were our companions here, many of them now departed and some gone forever. We think too of Evliya Çelebi, who has been our companion-guide for so long, and wonder what he might say if he could once again walk through the streets of his beloved town, so changed but so much the same.'

There is no easy answer to how we form an attachment to a place. The alchemy of attraction obeys its own weird formula. John's ability to share his love for a city, for those he knew and for what was and what had been, was a skilful act of persuasion, and one that puzzles me still.

Introduction

I FIRST CAME TO ISTANBUL in 1960 to teach at Robert College, an American school founded in 1863 on the European shore of the Bosphorus, the surpassingly beautiful strait that separates Europe and Asia in northwestern Turkey. With me were my wife, Toots (Dolores), and our three small children, Maureen, Eileen and Brendan. We stayed on until 1976, by which time the school had become a Turkish institution known as Boğazici Üniversitesi, or Bosphorus University. The children had by then gone off to school, and Toots and I moved in turn to Athens, Boston, London and Venice. But in 1993, the children having grown up and embarked upon their own lives, Toots and I returned to Istanbul and I resumed my post at the university, where I am still teaching today.

Istanbul had changed profoundly during the seventeen years of our absence, and I hardly recognised the city. Many old friends had passed away and I encountered their ghosts wherever I went. And that was why I decided to write this book, so that the exceptional people I had known, and the lost city in which we had lived, would not be forgotten.

Stamboul Ghosts is based almost entirely on my memory of departed friends of our early years, whose shades still speak to me from beyond the grave, as did the comrades of Odysseus when he met them in the Underworld, the Land of Dreams. It is an evocation of my departed Istanbul friends, who reappear to me from the night of time in the lost city I once knew.

John Freely, Istanbul, 2015

CHAPTER I

DEATH OF A GHOST

A FEW DAYS after we arrived in Istanbul I was walking along the European shore of the Bosphorus with my son, Brendan, on my shoulders. He was just sixteen months old, with a mop of blond curls that caught the equinoctial morning sunshine in a golden nimbus about his head, so that I must have looked like St Christopher carrying the Christ Child.

Just then I heard someone calling from one of the seaside houses above the embankment across the road: 'Good morning, sunny boy!' I looked up and saw a figure waving to us from the balcony of my friend the painter Seniye Fenmen's studio. Seniye came out and waved to me too, inviting me up for a coffee, so I crossed the road with Brendan and walked up the steps to her studio – where incidentally Toots would soon begin taking painting lessons. And that was how I came to meet Oğuz Halûk Alplaçin, better known as Hayalet, or The Ghost.

Oğuz was having his first rakı of the day, but it was a bit early for me, so I had a coffee with Seniye while she introduced me to my new friend, who had seated Brendan beside him on a wicker chair. There was room for both of them, since Hayalet was as thin as a wafer. One of the reasons he was called a ghost, Seniye said, was that when standing sideways to the sun he hardly cast a shadow. He also happened to be a professional ghostwriter, as well as a translator and writer of movie scripts, and a poet – though a group of his contemporaries once named him 'the worst poet in Istanbul, possibly

DEATH OF A GHOST 25

in the world'. He translated all Mickey Spillane's crime novels, and when he had finished those in print he wrote more of them under Spillane's name. He got away with it until Spillane sued him – though unsuccessfully, thanks to the state of Turkish law on intellectual property at the time.

Oğuz and I became good friends, which puzzled both his friends and mine, for we came from two quite different worlds. But that was precisely what drew us together. Toots liked him too, and he joined us in all our gatherings – parties at our house and evenings in town – and he and I would often meet at drinking places frequented by Istanbul's alcoholic intellectuals in Beyoğlu, Levantine Pera, the old Latin Quarter.

Oğuz was very interested in Ireland and borrowed a number of my books on Irish history and literature, as well as recordings of Irish music, which he never returned. During our first spring in Istanbul, Toots and I gave a St Patrick's Day party at our house, and we invited Oğuz, who brought along a couple of drunken Turkish poets. The same thing happened the next year and in the years that followed, and each time there seemed to be more drunken poets. Then one year a drunken poet came up to me and asked, 'Where fucking host?' I'd had enough, so the following year we decided to go to a St Patrick's Day party given by our friends Terry and Eileen Dunne. When we arrived home at four in the morning we found Oğuz sitting on our front steps with half-a-dozen drunken friends, whom I assumed to be poets, all of them looking very morose. Oğuz gave me a reproachful look and said, 'Freely, you're some fucking kind of traitor!' After which he and his friends left, walking down the graveyard road to the Bosphorus.

That summer, while we were off on the Greek island of Naxos, our daughter Maureen and her fiancé, Paul Spike, lived in our house. When we returned at the end of the summer we learned that Oğuz had died of cirrhosis – the fate of most of my bohemian Turkish friends at the time – and had been buried in the Aşiyan cemetery, just below our house. At the burial, when according to Muslim custom the imam called out asking for the name of the deceased's mother, no one knew it, for Oğuz had never spoken of his origins. Then one of his women friends shouted 'Eve!', whereupon he was lowered into the grave.

Apparently his drunken friends, those who had accompanied him to our St Patrick's Day parties, had decided to give him a traditional Irish wake, for that evening Maureen and Paul heard a group of drunks coming up the graveyard road to our house, where they stopped to sing Irish songs in very heavy Turkish accents.

One of my Turkish friends had saved an obituary from the newspaper *Milliyet*, entitled 'Death of a Ghost', written by a young journalist who had not known Oğuz but who had been intrigued by the Hayalet Oğuz myth that had developed in bohemian Pera. He had been with the group that had participated in the wake, which ended in Oğuz's sparsely furnished one-room apartment at the Afrika Han in Pera. There he found a bookcase filled with books about Ireland, and looking through them he noticed that they all belonged to a certain John Freely. His obituary ended with the question: 'Who is John Freely?'

The myth of Oğuz the Ghost lived on. Years later I was interviewed by two young Turkish film-makers who were making a documentary about Hayalet Oğuz. The myth had now developed to the point where Oğuz was taking the form of a real ghost, so that it was believed he had left no image in a mirror or on photographic film – a belief supported by the fact that there were no known photographs of him. The film-makers heard that I had known Oğuz well and asked if I could help. I looked through our albums and found a photo of him sitting with us and our friends at Bohem, a Greek taverna in Beyoğlu. The resulting documentary, which won a national award, shows me holding the album open at the photograph of Oğuz sitting beside me.

A couple of years later my friend Sezer Duru and her husband, Orhan, wrote a book called *O Pera'daki Hayalet* (*The Ghost of Pera*), which made the myth of Oğuz as the archetypal bohemian of Beyoğlu a permanent part of the lore of literary Istanbul in the early 1960s.

And so it went on. At a St Patrick's Day party in 1991 our dear friends Roddy and Olga O'Connor gave us a book of Irish revolutionary songs bearing my name. They had found it at a second-hand book market in Pendik, a coastal town in the Asian suburbs of Istanbul, and they noted this in their dedication. Then, on the page after their dedication, I saw another dedication: 'To John and Dolores, St Patrick's Day, 1962, Peter and Rosemary Shiras.' So it appeared that this was one of the books Oğuz had walked off with, which after his death had ended up in the market in Pendik, probably having passed through the hands of his friends. I occasionally checked the Sahaflar Çarşısı, the ancient second-hand book market in Istanbul, on the off-chance that another of my books on Ireland would turn up one day. For nothing ever really disappears in Istanbul, as I wrote in my (unpublished) book *The Broken-Down Paradise*, referring to the old Bit Pazarı, or Flea Market:

'Every great city has its flea market, but perhaps the one here surpasses them all, for the simple reason that most material objects are used for far longer in Stamboul than elsewhere, because of the lack of new things to buy. Nothing is ever thrown away, but is repaired or mended, passed on, traded, resold or stolen, perhaps acquiring a new identity as part of a composite of cannibalised components, passing and re-passing through the Bit Pazarı, which thus acts as a kind of second-hand heart in the circulatory system of junk which is Stamboul.'

The story of the book of Irish revolutionary songs holds even more poignancy now, since both the Shirases and the O'Connors have passed away, joining Oğuz and most of my other friends of Istanbul past in what Homer called the 'Land of Dreams'.

A few years ago I gave a talk at the Istanbul Book Fair. Among those present was my old friend Ömer Uluç, the painter, sole survivor of the bohemian circle of which Hayalet Oğuz has become the archetype. After the talk Ömer came up to me and said, 'John, you are Istanbul's memory.' And now Ömer has passed away too, joining almost all the others I knew when I first came to Istanbul – ghosts of the lost city that now exists only in my memory, for it has changed profoundly. But though I am mortal, the city is not, as if it had an immortal soul. Or so I believe. As Petrus Gyllius remarked in *The Antiquities of Constantinople*, published in the sixteenth century: 'While other cities are mortal, this one will remain as long as there are men on earth.'

Opposite: Oğuz the Ghost, by Gürdal Duyar, 20 August 1970

CHAPTER 2

QUEEN OF PERA

THE MAIN AVENUE of Beyoğlu is İstiklâl Caddesi, the old Grand' Rue de Pera, which extends from Taksim Square through Galatasaray Square to Tünel, the upper entrance to the funicular railway whose lower terminus is near the Galata Bridge. Joseph von Hammer, the nineteenth-century Austrian historian of the Ottoman Empire, once wrote of the old Grand' Rue that it was 'as narrow as the intellect of its inhabitants, and as long as the tapeworm of their intrigue'.

The first European embassies to the Sublime Porte were built on or near the Grand' Rue de Pera. The one closest to Tünel is the old Swedish Embassy, established here in its present building towards the end of the seventeenth century. Directly across the avenue from that is an ancient building known as the Narmanlı Yurdu, distinguished by its colonnade of Doric columns and the semicircular balcony at the corner of the *piano nobile*. This originally housed the old Russian Embassy, until they moved to a new building down the avenue in 1837. The Narmanlı Yurdu, which appears to date from the mid-eighteenth century, is now abandoned and slated for restoration. Up until 1976 it housed a congeries of shops, storerooms, offices, workshops and ateliers.

It was also for many years the residence of Aliye Berger-Boronai, whose apartment was on the *piano nobile*, opening off the semicircular balcony where, as she once told me, she used to sit and watch the night people of Pera passing.

Toots and I first met her early in the autumn of 1960, when we accompanied our Robert College friends David and Minnie Garwood to a big party given by Aliye in her apartment, where she had been living since the last days of the Ottoman Empire. Aliye's home was the madcap centre of bohemian Beyoğlu, a gathering place for eccentric and alcoholic artists, writers and composers, many of whom I met for the first time that evening, beginning friendships that lasted for many years and usually ended when one or another of them drank himself to death. Aliye herself became a close friend of ours, and she drew us into the bohemian world that swirled around her until the day she died. There were those of us who would have had Aliye's apartment declared a national monument, where she would reign forever as Queen of old Pera.

When we first met Aliye she was approaching sixty, but she was still unusually beautiful in a regal Ottoman way. Her father, Mehmed Şakir Pasha, had been Ottoman ambassador to Athens, and her uncle, Cevat Şakir Pasha, had served as grand vizier under Abdülhamid II. Her mother was a Greek-speaking Muslim from Crete and never really learned Turkish, Aliye told me. Her older brother, Cevat Şakir Kabaağaçlı, shot and killed their father during an argument in 1914 and served seven years in prison. Later, because of his political views, he was exiled to Bodrum, where his writing made him famous as the Halikarnas Balıkçısı, the Fisherman of Halicarnassus. Her older sister, Princess Fahrelnissa Zeid, wife of the Emir Zeid of Iraq, was a world-famous painter. One of Aliye's nieces, Füreya Koral, was a distinguished ceramicist; another niece, Şirin Devrim, was a well-known actress; and a nephew, Cem Kabaağaçlı, was a talented artist who did many of his paintings on boards ripped from the Şakir Konak, the family mansion on Büyükada, Greek Prinkipo, the largest and most beautiful of the Princes Isles, Istanbul's suburban archipelago in the Sea of Marmara.

One particular evening comes to mind when I think of Aliye's parties. Toots and I had arrived rather late, and we had trouble finding our way through the unlit labyrinth of hallways leading to her apartment. As we eventually approached her door we saw half-a-dozen people standing outside, apparently waiting to get in. We stood behind them. They were silent and didn't move. Only when I touched one of them did I realise it was a life-sized statue, as were the other figures. So I took Toots by the hand and led her past them and into the apartment, which was as usual packed with people. Aliye came over to greet us and laughed when I told her what had happened. A sculptor friend of hers had been evicted from his studio, she said, and had asked her to store his statues until he found another place. She had asked him to put them outside her door, so that if a thief came during the night he would think, just as I had, that they were guests waiting to enter her apartment, and that this would frighten him off.

Toots and I were the last to leave that evening, and we helped Aliye clean up. We learned that it was her habit to tip all the half-empty wine glasses into a huge vase of flowers on her dining-room table, from which she would serve the first of her guests to arrive at the next party. They were usually so drunk already that it didn't matter to them, she said. Aliye poured us what she called a 'night's cap' from the last bottle of wine, and we sat out with her on the balcony to watch the night people of Beyoğlu, some of whom waved up to Aliye as they passed along the old Grand' Rue de Pera.

One afternoon I called on Aliye to pick up an engraving we had bought from her, and it was then that I first learned how she had come to live in this apartment. During the last days of the Ottoman Empire, in the brief reign of Caliph Abdülmecid Efendi (1922–24), Aliye had been invited to Dolmabahçe Palace to attend a recital by the Hungarian violinist Şarl (Carl/Karolyi) Berger-Boronai, with whom, so she told me, she fell madly in love. Abdülmecid Efendi had hired Şarl to be his violin teacher, setting him up in this apartment in the Narmanlı Yurdu, and Aliye moved in as his mistress. She told me that several days a week a coach and four would appear outside the apartment to conduct Şarl to the palace for the Caliph's violin lessons. But then, on 3 March 1924, five months after the founding of the Turkish Republic, the Caliphate was abolished and Abdülmecid Efendi was given less than a day's notice before he and his family were sent off into exile, never to return.

Apparently Abdülmecid had secretly been composing a violin piece that he had planned to play to surprise his teacher, but his sudden departure

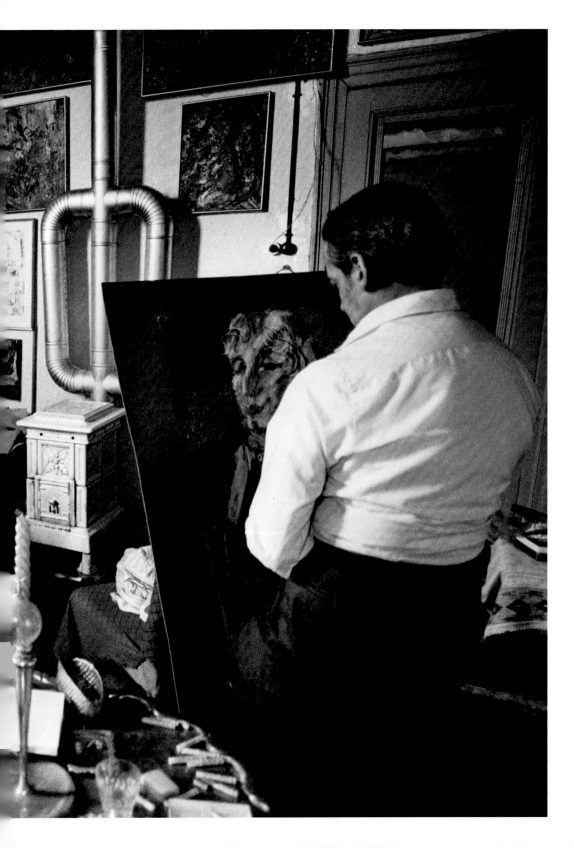

prevented him from doing so. He must have given it to Şarl just before leaving, however, because Aliye had a copy in her apartment, and one evening she lent it to me and Donald Hoffman, who taught music at Robert College. Donald arranged for the piece, entitled *Elegies*, to be played one evening at Robert College's Albert Long Hall by Professor Zerkin, our daughter Eileen's violin teacher. He had been a friend of Şarl, as were many of those in the audience, which may have been the last gathering of the old Ottoman elite. Aliye was sitting next to me during the recital, holding my hand, and I could feel the emotion welling up within her as the melancholic piece went on. But she retained her composure, and when *Elegies* ended she stood up with the rest of us and applauded Professor Zerkin, whose long and distinguished career ended with this recital.

From Aliye herself and other sources I pieced together the story of her tragic romance with Şarl, which, like the Gordian knot, apparently has no end, because the end of the rope is hidden within the knot itself.

After Abdülmecid Efendi's departure, Şarl and Aliye continued to live on in the apartment in the Narmanlı Yurdu, where Şarl supported them by giving violin lessons while Aliye began painting. In summer they lived in the Şakir Konak, the family mansion on Prinkipo. They didn't marry, but that didn't matter, Aliye said, for she was divinely happy with him.

But then in 1944, after twenty years of living with Şarl, she discovered he was having an affair with one of his students, an Armenian girl named Mayda Şahbaz, who lived with her mother in Moda, an Asian suburb of Istanbul. One evening Aliye took the pistol with which her brother Cevat had killed their father thirty years before, and went to Moda. Standing on a hillside in the park opposite Mayda's house, she saw Mayda and Şarl together in the bedroom. She knocked on the door with the pistol. Mayda's mother answered and Aliye could see Şarl and Mayda coming down the stairs. Aliye fired at them, but hit Mayda's mother, wounding her slightly in the arm before she slammed the door shut and locked it. Aliye then ran to the park across the street and sat on a bench, weeping hysterically, still holding the pistol. The police came and disarmed her, then took her to the police station, where she spent the night in jail. Charged with attempted homicide, she remained in jail while the case went through the courts. Thanks to the great influence of the Şakir family, the charges were dropped and Aliye was freed.

Aliye recuperated at the *konak* on Büyükada, until eventually she and Şarl were reconciled and they returned to their apartment in the Narmanlı Yurdu, where they resumed their old lives. Mayda Şahbaz, meanwhile, fled and went into hiding in Florya, a suburb of Istanbul on the European shore of the Sea of Marmara, where later in 1944 she gave birth to a son, whom she named Şarl after his father – as I was to learn eighteen years later when I met Şarl Shahbaz for the first time.

Aliye and Şarl Berger-Boronai were finally married in 1947, as she told me one evening, showing me their wedding photo. But then, in the sixth month of their marriage, Şarl died of a sudden heart attack as they were about to board the ferry from Büyükada to Istanbul. 'Freely,' she said, trying to hold back the tears, 'he died in my arms on the pier in Prinkipo.'

After Şarl's death Aliye had no desire to live, she told me. She tried to commit suicide, but failed. Her sister, Fahrelnissa Zeid, took her to live in London and introduced her to engraving, which she took to with a passion that restored her will to live. Aliye returned to the apartment in the Narmanlı Yurdu and began a new life there, gaining renown as a highly original artist, her engaging personality and boundless hospitality making her home the social centre of bohemian Beyoğlu.

Aliye became an important part of our lives, too. We invited her for supper one evening in the autumn of 1962, but she got the date wrong and came when Toots and I were out at a dinner party. We arrived home to find Aliye having a party with the children, riding around the living room on Brendan's tricycle. We had been in Spain the previous summer, and Maureen had done a painting of a flamenco dancer, which Aliye framed, with an inscription on the back reading 'Maureen Freely, great artist'.

Later that autumn a young man walked into my office in the Physics Department at Robert College, introducing himself as Şarl Şahbaz. The illegitimate son of Şarl Berger-Boronai and Mayda Şahbaz and I became good friends, and over the years I learned from him more bits and pieces of the romantic triangle involving his father and mother and Aliye, whom he adored – for after his father's death she had learned of

his existence and sought him out, bestowing as much love on him as if he were her own son.

Şarl, who has just turned seventy, now lives in Copenhagen and is a film-maker. He usually comes to Istanbul every year and looks me up, and we always talk about Aliye and Mayda, who came to see us once. Şarl is writing a novel entitled *Mayda*, and from the fragments he has sent me I keep learning more about the lost world of this Levantine romance, just as he learns from me through my indelible memories of Aliye. One evening a few years ago, Şarl and I were walking along the old Grand' Rue de Pera. As we passed the bow-shaped balcony of Aliye's old apartment in the Narmanlı Yurdu, Şarl looked up and said, 'I think I was conceived up there.'

Aliye died in her family *konak* on Büyükada on 9 August 1974. We were away on Naxos at the time and l learned of her death only after we returned to Istanbul a month later. Our friend the journalist Ann Bruno had been looking after Aliye during her last illness, and one evening after our return she told me of her final moments. Aliye's doctor had not allowed her to drink alcohol during her illness, but as her end neared she whispered to Ann, asking her for a sip of cognac. Ann brought her the cognac, which she drank. And then she said, 'Tell Freely not to forget me.' With that she passed away.

Toots and I went out to Büyükada soon afterwards to make a pilgrimage to Aliye's grave, in the Turkish cemetery on the slope of Mount Christos, northernmost of the island's two hills. The Şakir Konak was farther down the hill, and we walked there afterwards to take a last look, for it was to be replaced by a modern building. I remembered Aliye telling me how as a girl she always knew spring had arrived when she would see a great white cloud of storks soaring in from the south in their thousands to the summit of Mount Christos, where they caught the thermals and slowly spiralled upwards before continuing northward. One year they arrived during the night, and Aliye awoke in the morning to the sound of the clattering of thousands of beaks coming from the summit of Christos.

We were now nearing the autumnal equinox, and – as if in an epiphany putting us in touch with the spirit of Aliye – we watched as a flight of storks headed towards us from the north, then hovered over the peak of Christos before spiralling up and soaring southwards along the meridian.

Later that autumn we were invited to a gathering of Aliye's friends at her apartment in the Narmanlı Yurdu, so that we could all see it for the last time before it was closed and her belongings taken away. It had been her last request that a scholarship be founded in her name to enable young Turkish artists to study abroad, and some of those who had come to this gathering had formed a committee to try and carry out her wish.

Toots and I were the last to arrive, and I nodded to those I knew as we all stood there in silence in Aliye's salon – for me still filled with her ebullient presence. The most poignant reminder was the huge vase on the dining-room table, still filled with long-dead flowers and the remnants from the wine glasses that Aliye had emptied into it at the end of her last party. I looked across the room and saw that Sabahattin Bey, the former director of the Haghia Sophia Museum, was staring at the vase too. Our eyes met for a moment and he smiled faintly at me, sharing a precious memory of Aliye.

Many years later, caught in a sudden shower as I was walking along the old Grand' Rue de Pera, I took cover in the arcade at the entrance to the courtyard of the Narmanlı Yurdu. When the shower had passed I walked into the courtyard and looked up to where Aliye's apartment had been. I stood there for a while, gazing that way, thinking of her.

I was soon joined by the old man who owned the second-hand bookshop at the rear of the courtyard, a member of the Ottoman aristocracy whom I recalled seeing at some of Aliye's parties. He stood beside me for a few moments in silence, looking in the same direction. Without turning, he said to me, in Turkish, 'You're looking at Aliye Hanım's apartment, aren't you?' I nodded, and the two of us stood there in silence, each reflecting on our own memories of Aliye, our uncrowned Queen of Pera.

CHAPTER 3

GHOSTS IN EXILE

T HE ISLAND OF BÜYÜKADA (Greek Prinkipo), has long been a
place of exile, both forced and self-imposed. During the medieval
Byzantine period, deposed or retired emperors and empresses
lived out their last years in monasteries and convents they had
founded on the island, supposedly spending their days fasting and their
nights in prayer. During the Ottoman period, deposed sultans were usually
either executed or imprisoned in the palace of Topkapı in the Old City,
while Büyükada became the residence of choice of mostly upper-class
Greeks, Armenians, Sephardic Jews and the Turkish elite, such as the Şakir
family, many of whom continue to live here as a refuge from the tumultuous
life of the great imperial city on the sunset horizon.

The most notable exile on Büyükada in Republican times was Leon
Trotsky. He lived there from 1929 to 1933, after being exiled from Russia,
and it was here that he wrote his autobiography and began his three-
volume *History of the Russian Revolution*. Trotsky describes his exile on
Büyükada in an essay entitled 'Farewell to Prinkipo', written soon after he
left the island:

> Prinkipo is an island of peace and forgetfulness. The life of
> the world reaches here after long delays and hushed down…
> Prinkipo is a fine place to work with a pen, particularly during
> autumn and winter when the island becomes completely
> deserted and woodcocks appear in the park. Not only are

there no theatres here, but no movies. Automobiles are forbidden. Are there many such places in the world? In our house we have no telephone. The braying of the donkey acts soothingly upon the nerves. One cannot forget for a moment that Prinkipo is an island, for the sea is under the window, and there is no hiding from the sea at any point in the island. Ten metres away from the stone fence we catch fish, at fifty metres – lobsters. For weeks at a time the sea is calm as a lake.

Trotsky left Büyükada on 17 July 1933, never to return. Despite his isolation, he seems to have enjoyed his exile, as evidenced by the last entry in his notebook, on the day he departed: 'It has been four-and-a-half years. I have the strange feeling of having my feet firmly planted on Büyükada.'

Another exile from that period was of a quite different type, if indeed his stay on Büyükada can be called an exile at all. This was Archbishop Angelo Roncalli, later to become Pope John XXIII, who in 1934 became Papal Nuncio to Greece and Turkey, based in Istanbul, with his summer residence at the Nuncio's mansion on Büyükada. Clerical gossip had it that Roncalli was sent off to Istanbul by his enemies in the Vatican, who wanted this formidable personage as far from Rome as possible. But Roncalli made the best of his exile and became an extremely popular figure in Istanbul, regularly going to the theatre and the opera, as well as diplomatic receptions, since a Papal Nuncio has the rank of ambassador.

At the age of sixty-four, in 1944, Roncalli was appointed to the difficult post of Nuncio to Paris, which had just been liberated from German occupation. While there he once said: 'You know, it's rough being a Papal Nuncio. I get invited to these diplomatic affairs where everyone stands around with a small plate of canapés trying not to look bored. Then in walks a shapely woman in a low-cut, revealing gown, and everyone in the whole place turns around and looks – at me!'

During our early years in Istanbul, Roncalli was still remembered with affection on Büyükada, and locals pointed out his residence with pride. The Şakir Konak stood just beside the Nuncio's mansion, and Aliye Berger-Boronai knew Roncalli. She told us how her bedroom overlooked the

Nuncio's garden, and how on summer mornings she would look down to see Roncalli walking around the flowerbeds, reciting his daily office in loud, eloquent Latin while a fat little Dominican friar followed behind him playing the violin.

Not far from the Şakir mansion there lived a self-imposed exile from the past, an old woman whose tiny house I was shown by Avadis Hacınlıyan, an Armenian student of mine at Robert College who had been born and grown up on Büyükada. This venerable lady was the last known survivor of the harem of Abdülhamid II, which had been disbanded when the Sultan was deposed in 1909. She took refuge on Büyükada, known only to her neighbours, who called her Saraylı Hanım, 'the Palace Lady'.

Avadis said he had seen her once or twice as a boy, when she would briefly open her door to buy something from a passing pedlar. She was still living there when Avadis gave me a tour of the island in 1964, but when I passed her house a few years later I learned that she had passed away, though no one knew where she was buried, as though she was a ghost.

Avadis also showed me the residence of another departed exile, the Castle of Dr Hintiryan, high on the eastern slope of Mount Christos. A castle it was indeed, complete with crenellated battlements, watchtowers, turrets, a barbican and a moat crossed by a drawbridge. But as we approached to take a closer look I realised that the whole edifice was a fantastic fake, constructed entirely of flimsy, unpainted wood, now falling to pieces. Yellowed newspapers were flapping in its shuttered windows, birds flitted through holes in its warped and rickety walls, its moat was dry and filled with debris and garbage, including piles of broken wine bottles.

Avidis told me the extraordinary story of the castle and its owner, just as he had heard it from his grandfather. This medieval-style monstrosity, he said, was built towards the end of the nineteenth century by Dr Hintir Hintiryan, an Armenian dentist who had retired to Büyükada after fleeing various scandals in Stamboul. Avadis well remembered his grandfather's tales of the strange goings-on at the castle.

Dr Hintiryan, it seems, had fallen victim to the same mania that had seized Cervantes's hero, for he believed himself to be a chivalrous knight errant, long after the age of chivalry was over. Thus he built this medieval castle – in wood, since time and money were in short supply, though not imagination. And as his faithful servant – every Don Quixote must have his Sancho Panza – he hired a simple-minded fisherman named Hagop. The dentist dressed himself and his man-at-arms in medieval costumes, purchased from a theatrical supply house, and set himself up as a knight in his castle, ready to challenge all comers and to succour damsels in distress. But no comers ever came to the wooden castle, and certainly no distressed damsels, so Dr Hintiryan spent his time carousing by himself in what passed for his great hall, flinging empty wine bottles through the castle windows into the moat. Poor Hagop, while not serving his master at table, stood at his post on the crenellated battlements, dressed in his papier mâché armour, armed with a tin sword and a cardboard shield, faithfully calling out the hours of his watch and proclaiming that all was well along the walls. And so the dentist spent his last years on Büyükada, a mad and alcoholic knight errant in the wrong century.

I asked if Dr Hintiryan was buried in the Armenian cemetery on Büyükada, but Avadis said that he wasn't, having been excommunicated by the Armenian Orthodox Church. He certainly would not have been buried in the Turkish, Greek or Jewish cemeteries on Büyükada or in Istanbul either, for these received only the departed of their own faiths, as if each had its own suburb in the next world. Thus Dr Hintiryan fell into the same category as Penelope's unburied suitors, slaughtered by Odysseus on his return to Ithaca, who ended up as ghosts in the Underworld.

There was one other extraordinary Büyükada exile, whom I came to know in the early 1960s, though only for a few unforgettable hours. Toots and I would occasionally spend a weekend on the island, at a raffish *pansiyon* called Villa Rıfat, about halfway along the eastern shore. One afternoon, while Toots took a nap, I went for a stroll along the coast road, heading south. I soon fell into step with a white-bearded ancient, whom I first assumed to be an old dervish, trudging along the road lugging two large burlap sacks, a tattered turban on his grizzled head, garbed in a threadbare US Army overcoat and shod in sandals made from discarded automobile tires. I greeted him in Turkish, and was flabbergasted when he responded in excellent but somewhat archaic English, with just a hint of what I guessed was an Austrian accent.

As we walked along, he told me about himself and how he came to live here on Prinkipo, as he called it. His name was Franz Fischer, and in the late 1930s he had been a professor of biology at the University of Istanbul. But at the start of the Second World War in 1939 he had turned his back on modern civilisation in disgust and fled to Prinkipo, building himself a little shack on the sparsely inhabited southern end of the island, where he had lived ever since.

Islanders we passed along the road greeted him as Kaya Baba. 'Baba' is the name given to a venerable old man, or to a saint, and from the reverent manner in which the locals spoke to Franz I gathered that they believed him to be saintly, all the more so since he was eccentric, 'touched by Allah'. He stopped now and then along the road to sell the eggs he was carrying in one of his two sacks; the other, he explained, contained feed he had bought at the market for the chickens and pigeons who were his only companions.

Franz and I quickly became good friends, for despite the difference in our backgrounds, our ways of thinking were remarkably similar. He apologised for what he said was his poor English, which was actually very good, though interspersed here and there with phrases in German, French, Greek, Armenian, Turkish and Ladino, the language the local Sephardic Jews had brought with them when they were evicted from Spain by Ferdinand and Isabella. Franz excused himself by saying I was the first foreigner he had spoken to in all the years of his self-imposed exile from the modern world.

When we came to the southern end of the island, Franz invited me into his home, a ramshackle wooden hovel which also housed a chicken coop and dovecote. We sat down on two egg crates and he served me tea, made over an open fire, as he again apologised, this time for the primitive accommodation, for I was the first guest he had ever invited into his home.

Franz told me that what he had missed most during his self-imposed exile was the opportunity to converse with someone like myself who could appreciate his philosophy and poetry – whereupon he opened an old trunk and took out two parcels wrapped in newspaper and plastic sheeting. These, he said, contained the two tomes on which he had worked throughout much of his adult life. Both were neatly written in pencil. The first one he showed me was in German. This was his *Aethergeist*, or *Spirit of the Aether*, a work of pantheistic philosophy which he proceeded to explain to me at length, ranting like an Old Testament prophet, his bright blue eyes blazing with messianic fervour. 'My philosophy is the product of my own mind,' he shouted, 'because during the years I was composing it my thought was uncontaminated by the falsehoods of others!'

His shouting disturbed the pigeons, so that they flew about in flapping coveys, while the hens started cackling and the cocks crowing. After they had calmed down Franz chuckled, showing me how his manuscript had become besmirched by bird droppings, some fresh and some old. 'I live with the birds, and in this way they give me their opinion of my philosophy,' he said, and we laughed so much that his eyes welled with tears.

When Franz opened the second volume his mood changed and he spoke in an elegiac tone, for this comprised the collected poetry of his lifetime. The poems were in chronological order, the first written in 1917 in northern Italy, on the Mezzolombardo front, on the eve of the battle of Caporetto, in which he had fought as an infantryman in the Austrian Army. Like Ernest Hemingway, he had been seriously wounded in the battle, and this experience, he said, had changed the course of his life.

After the war Franz returned to Vienna, his birthplace, but when Hitler came to power he fled to Romania and then emigrated to the US, where he found a job as a butler, working for a wealthy family on Park Avenue in New York City. At the same time he did evening graduate studies at New York University, just as I did in the 1950s, and received a doctorate in biology. He then accepted a post at the University of Istanbul, which he resigned in 1939 on the outbreak of war when he fled to Prinkipo.

The poetry had been composed throughout his long odyssey, the earlier verses in German, some of the later ones in English. They were written in places as far apart as the trenches in Caporetto, a coffee house in Vienna, a steamer on the Black Sea and the New York subway. All expressed his transcendental feelings of universal love.

Coming to the end of the volume, I noticed that the last poem was written in 1953; entitled *Mesons and Melons*, it was dedicated to Werner Heisenberg, the German physicist who had won the Nobel Prize for his Uncertainty Principle and his formulation of quantum mechanics. As a physicist I understood the point Franz was making in this poem, which was that the melons growing in the fields on Prinkipo were made up of the same matter as the mesons and other fundamental subatomic particles discovered through the quantum mechanics formulated by Heisenberg and his contemporaries. He had sent a copy of the poem to Heisenberg, who had responded with a very gracious letter of thanks, which Franz showed to me with great pride.

I asked Franz why he had not written anything after this, and he paused for a moment before answering: 'I wrote no more since nothing has happened to me since then. I am at one with the universe and there is no longer any need to read or write.'

When I said goodbye to Franz and left his little shack he looked very sad, and so I tried to cheer him up by saying I would call on him when I came out to the island again. But years went by before Toots and I returned to Büyükada, and when I went to visit Franz I learned that he had passed away. No one seemed to know where he was buried. But it didn't really matter, for I knew that now he truly was at one with the universe. And so his ghost continues to live on in my memory.

CHAPTER 4

THE LIFE OF THE PARTY

ROBERT COLLEGE WAS FOUNDED by American missionaries, and when deciding whether to accept an offer of a teaching post there I was afraid it might still have a missionary character, particularly in its social life. But when I arrived, in 1960, I found that though some of the College community were with the American Board of Missions, and a few of the older faculty were missionary types, most of those who had started teaching at RC from the 1950s onward were not – particularly the 'Hill Crowd', as they were known, disapprovingly, by those who were not part of their circle.

David and Minnie Garwood were the earliest of the College community to establish themselves on the Hill, the eminence above the campus in Rumelihisarı where some of the older faculty houses had been built. David had started teaching at RC in 1939, just after graduating from Harvard. Minnie, who had been born in Rumelihisarı, was the daughter of Kaspar Tüygil, an Armenian who had graduated from RC in 1897 and served as College Librarian for more than half a century. Her mother, Armen, acted as matron of the school dormitory for many years. David and Minnie were married in 1948 and had three children – John, Ann and Vicky – who were about the same age as our three kids, so our two families were very close.

David had been on sabbatical leave at Princeton in the spring of 1960 when we first met him and Minnie. I was just completing my doctorate at New York University, where I had been studying at night since 1951, while I worked as a research physicist during the day, first at the US Army Signal

Corps Laboratory in Fort Monmouth, New Jersey, then at Princeton University. When I received my doctorate at NYU, I was offered a permanent position as a research physicist at Princeton, but it was after talking about Robert College with David and Minnie that I finally decided to accept a teaching position there instead. Minnie had quickly disabused us of our notion that RC might still have a missionary atmosphere with a story that she told us one evening.

It seems that before their marriage David had been living in one of the College houses with Hilary Sumner-Boyd, his colleague in the Humanities Department. They had invited everyone in the community to a Christmas party, and had cooked up a huge jug of home-made vodka in order to prepare eggnog and 'Hill Cocktails', as they were known by the Hill Crowd, for their guests. Unfortunately, lifting the jug onto a table on the balcony, they dropped it and it broke. All the vodka poured down the drain into the gutters of the cobbled street below, where the local cats and dogs were lapping it up as the first guests began arriving and its unmistakable smell pervaded the entire village, so that the missionary families knew the Hill Crowd were having another big party.

The first big College party we went to was given by Keith and Joanne Greenwood. They had arrived in Istanbul in 1950, Keith to teach in the Humanities Department at RC and Joanne at the American College for Girls. They married in 1951 and had three children, Tony, Debby and Brian, the same ages as our children and those of the Garwoods, so our three families formed close bonds that spanned two generations.

The Greenwoods threw the party to introduce us new arrivals to one another and to the old hands. Besides ourselves, the new faculty at the party were Donald (Buck) and Kay Rogers, and Floyd and Anne Couch. The old hands, besides the Garwoods, included Cal and Cary Atwood, and John (Sherry) and Diana Schereschewsky. The Atwoods and Schereschewskys had come to Istanbul in 1958, both Cal and Sherry to teach at Robert Academy, the secondary-school division of RC. They too had three children each, so between them and us and the Garwoods and Greenwoods there were fifteen children, who were always behind the scenes when their parents were giving a party, supposedly asleep in their rooms. Of course there was no way they could have slept, given the music, singing, loud conversation and laughter, and the older ones would take the occasional peek to see what was going on. This was certainly true of our daughter Maureen, and her second novel, *The Life of the Party*, is based on the college parties she witnessed or heard of during our early years in Istanbul. The principal male character in the novel is Hector Cabot, who, as Maureen recently told me, is a collage of Keith Greenwood, Cal Atwood, John Schereschewsky, Buck Rogers and Peter Pfeiffer, while Thomas Ashe, Hector's fun-loving friend, is me.

Not long afterwards, Toots and I threw our first party. At the time we were living in off-campus housing, in a villa at the upper end of the Arifi Paşa Korusu, a cobbled lane leading up from the Bosphorus. Our guests were all members of the Robert College community, including the Turkish poet Cevat Çapan, an alumnus of the college.

The party was well under way when Cevat appeared with the American writer James Baldwin, who had just arrived in Istanbul. Earlier that day I had read a short story of his in *The Atlantic* magazine – entitled 'This Morning, This Evening, So Soon' – about two young black couples in Paris just after the war. It was a custom of ours that anyone crashing one of our parties had to sing for his supper, so Maureen and Eileen marched Baldwin into the living room, where he stood up on a table and sang an old African American folk song called 'Tell Old Bill'. And then I realised where the title of his story came from.

> *Tell old Bill when he comes home this morning,*
> *Tell old Bill when he comes home this evening,*
> *Tell old Bill when he comes home*
>   *to leave them downtown gals alone*
> *This morning, this evening, so soon.*

Jimmy, as everyone called him, quickly shifted the party into high gear, and it was nearly dawn before the last guests went home. Jimmy was the last to leave, and the two of us had a nightcap on the balcony, talking and comparing notes about our past lives, which had been very different but with many elements in common. He was a couple of years older than me, but we had both grown up poor in New York during the same period, he in Harlem and me in Brooklyn. He had been a shoeshine boy and worked in a sweatshop, whereas I had been a scavenger and worked in a condom factory. Jimmy had left the US and made a new life in France, just as Toots and I were doing in Turkey.

We finished our nightcaps as the sun rose above the hills of Asia across the Bosphorus, with the first call to prayer echoing from both sides of the straits along with the clamour of barking dogs and crowing roosters. Jimmy got up to go, smiling his brilliant toothy smile as he said, 'We've come a long way, buddy!'

My friend Murat Belge, a reveller at many of the parties on the Hill, had *The Life of the Party* translated into Turkish, giving it the title *Eğlence Bitti*, which means 'The Party's Over'. Murat undoubtedly chose that title because he thought the world of Maureen's novel was now gone for ever. But today, as I stroll around the campus of the university, past the houses where we and our friends once lived, I still hear faint echoes of the music and laughter bubbling up from the house of memory, where the party still goes on.

Opposite: 'The Bosphorus', by Aliye Berger-Boronai (1903–74)

CHAPTER 5

PETER PFEIFFER MEMORIAL
GOOSE-BUYING DAY

P ETER PFEIFFER WAS A MAN of three nationalities and two personalities, liable to switch from one passport or mood to another, depending on circumstances and how much he'd had to drink, when he sometimes became what Scandinavians call a 'berserker', the Old Norse warrior who went into battle in a drug-induced trance. Peter's trances were induced by drink, not drugs, and when he went berserk he never hurt anyone, for he always passed out before he did any damage, awakening with no memory of where he had been or what he had done.

Peter had joined the Robert College faculty in 1960 as Professor of Civil Engineering, with a degree from Berlin University. He had been born in Norway, with Norwegian citizenship, and after the Second World War had moved with his family to Berlin, where they became citizens of the East German Republic. Then, after marrying his wife Maya, he acquired Finnish nationality.

Travelling in Europe, Peter carried all three of his passports with him, particularly when visiting his parents in East Berlin. His father was a famous sculptor, and whenever Peter visited, using either his Norwegian or his Finnish passport, he would manage to smuggle out one of the very valuable statuettes his family had been hiding from the authorities. He had been visiting them in the summer of 1961, as the Berlin Wall was being erected, when he tried to smuggle out another of his father's sculptures. Arriving very drunk at Checkpoint Charlie, he was searched

PETER PFEIFFER MEMORIAL DAY 63

and the statuette confiscated – along with all three of his passports. Under interrogation he told the authorities that he was working for an American school in Turkey – which so confused them that Peter was able to talk his way out of the situation, using his drunkenness as an excuse.

Before coming to Robert College, Peter had spent several years working for an American construction firm in India, where his work had once taken him to Lahore. One day, while on a bender there, he decided to go to a bordello – purely because the rhyming of the words 'whore' and 'Lahore' amused him. But the police raided the place and arrested him for being drunk and disorderly, which he knew was just a pretext to extract a big bribe.

Peter and Maya had met Jimmy Baldwin at our party and they became good friends. That spring they gave a big party at their house, which was just below ours on a cobbled lane leading off the Arifi Paşa Korusu. Maya was an artist, and so besides their friends from the College they had invited a number of Turkish artists, most notably Aliye Berger-Boronai, along with Jimmy Baldwin and his old friend, the famous American journalist and author Emily Hahn, known to her friends as Mickey.

I had read some of her articles in the *The New Yorker*, particularly those about China, where she had begun her career as a journalist. I talked with her for a while about China, where I had spent the last weeks of the Second World War as a US Navy commando attached to the Chinese Army, and we exchanged jokes about Chiang Kai-shek, whom General 'Vinegar Joe' Stillwell referred to as 'Peanut Brain'. I had also read her first book, *Seductio Ad Absurdum: The Principles & Practices of Seduction, A Beginner's Handbook*, a very funny work on how men try to seduce women.

While we were chatting she looked around and said, 'Where the hell is Jimmy?' At that moment we heard high-pitched laughter from the Judas tree above us, and we looked up to see Baldwin grinning down at us. He shook the tree so that Judas blossoms came showering over us, floating in our wine. She shouted up to him in mock anger. 'You bastard! I hate you. Not because you're a nigger, and not because you're a faggot, but because you're so fucking ugly!'

Peter was reasonably well behaved at that party, probably because he was the host, but also because he had his hands full with a number of drunken Turkish artists and an even more drunken American from the US Consulate, Chuck Waters, who insulted the wife of my friend, the artist Ömer Uluç, and started a fight with me, though he backed away when I squared up to him.

A couple of weeks later, to celebrate the blossoming of the Judas trees along the Bosphorus, we gave a champagne party. (Turkish champagne was almost undrinkable, but it cost the equivalent of about half an American dollar, so we bought a dozen cases for the party.) It was a beautiful evening, with a full moon sailing across the sky and nightingales singing their hearts out in the woods around us. When the party began winding down, some of my pals and I decided to take a moonlit swim in the Bosphorus while our wives enjoyed a nightcap on the balcony. Peter didn't join us – he had disappeared at some point in the evening – and Maya had gone home alone, having given up trying to find him.

After everyone had left, Toots and I were picking up the empty champagne bottles that had been left all over the apartment when one of them evaded my grasp and rolled behind the couch. I pulled the couch away from the wall to retrieve it, and it was then that I found Peter. He had apparently passed out, dead drunk, and fallen behind it. It took me a while to wake him up and get him to his feet. He seemed surprised that all the guests, including his wife, had left. I tried to explain that Maya had tried to find him, but had given up and gone home by herself. But Peter was convinced that she had gone with another man and was now with him in their house. He staggered out onto the balcony and began throwing champagne bottles at his house, just below ours – I could hear them smashing on the roof tiles and exploding like grenades as all our neighbours began putting on their lights to see what was going on. I got hold of him before he could cause any further damage, hoping no one had called the police, and managed to deliver him home to Maya. The two of us got him to bed, and he was soon sound asleep and snoring loudly.

Talking to Peter at a faculty meeting a few days later, I realised he had no memory of what had happened at the party. I assumed Maya hadn't reminded him that he'd gone berserk – perhaps because she was resigned to his behaviour, or perhaps because it was part of Finnish culture.

The Pfeiffers went back to Finland for the summer vacation, and when they returned in the fall they were accompanied by two Finnish couples who had acquired Turkish citizenship and rented apartments on the Bosphorus near them. Peter and Maya introduced them to us and their other College friends at a party and we found them very charming and a great deal of fun. But as the drink started flowing I could see that they too were berserkers, the women as well as the men, and even the Hill Crowd were impressed by their wildness. The two couples remained in Istanbul for only a few months before moving back to Finland – they found the Turkish lifestyle too restrained for their taste. So did Peter, I could tell, though his job as a full professor in the RC Engineering School required a certain decorum, so that he held himself in check – at least most of the time. When he did fall off the wagon it was with a resounding crash.

Peter's most memorable escapade occurred during the Christmas holiday season in 1961. He had gone to Beyoğlu on the morning of 22 December to buy two geese for their holiday dinner. Maya called me late in the afternoon to say that he had not returned, and she was worried something might have happened. I told her not to worry, that I would go downtown to look for him. I figured he was drinking at one of the meyhanes in and around the Galatasaray fish market, where he would have gone for the geese.

Peter wasn't in any of the drinking places in the fish market and I thought the only other place he might be was Rejans, the old White Russian restaurant in the Olivio Pasajı, a little alleyway off İstiklâl Caddesi. Rejans was renowned for its borscht, chicken Kiev and home-made lemon vodka, and Toots and I always went there after shopping in the fish market.

I saw Peter the moment I entered Rejans. He was sitting in a booth with Aliye, who waved to me in greeting. Peter sat there with two plucked geese slung over his shoulders, their legs tied together round his neck. He was glassy-eyed and his speech was slurred as he invited me to sit down with them, pouring me a lemon vodka and ordering another bottle. I told him Maya was waiting for him, so he called for the bill but wouldn't leave until we had finished off the vodka, by which time Aliye had gone, saying she was expecting guests for supper.

Peter was so drunk I had to support him as he staggered out of Rejans. It had started snowing while we were in the restaurant, and he kept slipping and falling as we walked down the Olivio Pasajı and out on to İstiklâl Caddesi. I tried to hail a cab, but they were all full, so we started up the avenue towards Taksim Square, where there was a taxi rank. But as we passed the passage leading to the Atlas Cinema, Peter said he had to go to the toilet. So we walked to the inner end of the passage and went into Kulis (Backstage), a café-bar frequented by actors from the Küçük Sahne (Little Theatre), where I stood at the bar and ordered a beer while Peter went back to the men's room.

By the time I had finished my beer Peter still hadn't returned, so I went in search of him, but the men's room attendant told me Peter had left five minutes before. I ran out onto İstiklâl but there was no sign of him, so I made the rounds of all the drinking places I knew in the area. But to no avail. Peter had given me the slip, and I finally gave up and took a taxi home, stopping to tell Maya what had happened. She shook her head and sighed in resignation. He would show up sooner or later, she said, and she would let me know when he returned.

Maya called me two days later, on Christmas Eve, asking me to come and help her with Peter, who had just come home. As I approached their house I could hear him shouting incoherently, and when Maya let me in I saw him lurching drunkenly around the living room, barefoot and stark naked except for a large Turkish flag wrapped around his waist. Before I could get hold of him, he staggered into the Christmas tree and knocked it over, after which he passed out and lay there snoring away, covered with shards of shattered glass baubles, flashing lights and decorations. Maya took the two geese off to the fridge, after which she covered Peter with a blanket and then poured two cups of eggnog. We wished one another Merry Christmas before I left and went home.

The next time I saw the Pfeiffers was the evening of 2 January, when Toots and I and the Hill Crowd went to a party at their house, along with some Turkish friends from town, most notably Aliye. Peter was very affable and charming, giving no indication of remembering his Christmas escapade. Toots and I were the last to leave, and as we were sipping our nightcaps he put on a recording that he knew was a favourite of mine and which he loved too: Paul Robeson singing 'The Banjo Song'. Whenever I hear the song now I think of Peter and that evening:

> *I plays de banjo better now*
> *Dan him dat taught me do,*
> *Because he plays for all de worl',*
> *An' I jes' plays for you…*

> *I never knows if dey will shine*
> *Wet wid tears or dew;*
> *I only know dat, dew or tears,*
> *Dey shine because of you.*
> *Dey shine because of you,*
> *Of you.*

Peter resigned from the College at the end of the academic year, when he and Maya and their children, Susan and Yussi, returned to Finland. During the following Christmas holiday a group of us from the College were having a few beers in the Çiçek Pasajı, while our wives were shopping for geese and turkeys in the fish market. Afterwards, at a late lunch in Rejans, we ordered the traditional borscht and chicken Kiev, along with a bottle of lemon vodka. I offered a toast to Peter Pfeiffer, and after we had drunk to him I related the story of his escapade the previous Christmas. Until then I had told no one except Toots, because it might have cost him his job – particularly his use of a Turkish flag to cover his nakedness.

I suggested we make this an annual ritual, which I dubbed Peter Pfeiffer Memorial Goose-Buying Day, and which we celebrated until Toots and I left Istanbul in 1976. When we returned in 1993 there was no one left from the original College crowd who had known Peter, so I celebrated the ritual by myself, along with the ghost of Peter Pfeiffer. For by then, as I learned from a friend, he had passed away. He had gone out fishing, it seems, taking along a bottle of vodka, and was last seen rowing out to sea, where he was enveloped in a fog bank and disappeared for ever.

Our daughter Maureen describes the goose-buying episode in *The Life of the Party*, attributing it to her principal character, Hector Cabot, along with the escapades of John Schereschewsky, Cal Atwood, Keith Greenwood and Buck Rogers – a heavy burden of misbehaviour for one man to bear, even a fictional character. But I am here to set the record straight that it was my berserker friend Peter Pfeiffer who bought the geese that Christmas in Istanbul. And when I meet his shade in Beyoğlu, he is drinking lemon vodka in Rejans with Aliye, a pair of geese slung over his shoulders.

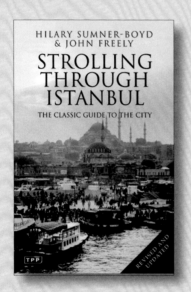

HILARY SUMNER-BOYD
& JOHN FREELY

STROLLING
THROUGH
ISTANBUL

THE CLASSIC GUIDE TO THE CITY

TPP

REVISED AND UPDATED

İstanbul Gezgininin Rehberi

İstanbul'u Dolaşırken

Strolling Through İstanbul

Hilary Sumner-Boyd / John Freely

Çeviren: Yelda Türedi

25. YIL
pan

CHAPTER 6

STROLLING
THROUGH ISTANBUL

O NE OF THE OLDER TEACHERS at Robert College whom I came to know early on was Hilary Sumner-Boyd, who had dual US and British citizenship and degrees from both Columbia and Oxford. Hilary had joined the faculty at Robert College as Professor of Humanities in 1943, and from then on he applied his formidable scholarship to a study of the antiquities of Istanbul entitled *The Seven Hills of Constantinople*, which he passed on to me at cocktail time in his study at least once a week. As time went by, I too began writing about Istanbul, a book I tentatively called *The Broken-Down Paradise*, which was very different from Hilary's work, since it was about the street life of Istanbul, past and present – lore I had picked up in both walking around the city and reading about it in the very rich collection of the College library.

One of the sources I used was the *Seyyahatnâme*, or *The Narrative of Travels*, written in the mid-seventeenth century by Evliya Çelebi, a Turkish chronicler who spent all his life describing his travels throughout the Ottoman Empire, with most of the first two volumes devoted to a description of Istanbul, his beloved birthplace. During my explorations of Istanbul, Evliya became my invisible companion guide, as I compared my town to his, as if we were strolling around it together, despite the four centuries that separated us. We seemed to share a deep love for the Old City that made me feel a kinship with him, as if his shade were conversing with me from beyond the grave.

Early in 1972 I was talking to my friend Bill Edmonds, editor of Redhouse Press, a publishing house run by the American Board of Missions. Bill had heard that both Hilary and I had been writing huge books on Istanbul, both of them as yet unpublished. He suggested we combine and condense our manuscripts so that Redhouse could publish our joint book as a scholarly guide to the city, for there was no adequate work of that kind on the market. When I talked about it that evening with Hilary, his response was, 'Why not, my dear?' Whereupon I informed Bill and he gave us the go-ahead.

Hilary described *Strolling* as a 'conflation' of our two books – which remain unpublished to the present day. Each evening I would walk over to his apartment after supper and we would shuffle our manuscripts together, while Hilary's Armenian housekeeper, Monik (dubbed 'Monik Depressive' by one of our friends), served us Hill Cocktails.

I organised the chapters into a series of strolls around Istanbul, which Toots and I would walk on Saturdays, and then again with Hilary once we thought we had each one right. After we'd finished a chapter I would call Bill Edmonds and he would drop by our house and pick it up, returning it that evening with his editorial comments, which he and I discussed over the usual succession of Hill Cocktails.

As *Strolling* progressed, Hilary and I got to know each other far better than we had before, and I began to learn things about him and his background that were not generally known in College circles. However, there were aspects of his past that I didn't discover until years after he had passed way, and even then there were lacunae in his story which continue to elude me.

Hilary's real name, I learned, was Carl Haywood, and he was the illegitimate son of William D (Big Bill) Haywood, one of the founders of International Workers of the World. Hilary, the name by which he seems to have been known since his youth, had been born in Boston, Massachusetts in 1910 and was educated privately there before taking a BA at Columbia University and an MA at Oxford, where he was a student at Christ Church. His nominal father, whose name I never learned, had known the journalist John Reed, and his mother appears to have been a friend of Leon Trotsky.

The famous philosopher AJ Ayer, with whom Hilary had been at Oxford, noted that he 'was the founder and so far as I know the only member of the Oxford Trotsky Society, and the ferocity of his political opinions was belied by the gentleness of his manner'.

During the years 1937–38 Hilary had been business manager of the Trotskyite newspaper *The Red Flag*, which he published out of his flat on Edgware Road in London, a centre for Trotskyite activities. Hilary wrote under the pseudonyms Sumner and Boyd, and subsequently legally changed his last name to Sumner-Boyd. After his death in 1976 his literary executor, Michael Austin, went through his papers and found a letter from Trotsky thanking him for the efforts he had made on his behalf.

None of this was known to the College administration, or to the Turkish authorities. If it had been, Hilary would not have been allowed to teach in Turkey, which was going through a political crisis at the time. The situation had degenerated into violent anarchy, and left-wing students denounced RC's American administration as an example of 'cultural imperialism', demanding that the school be taken over by the Turkish Government. The anarchy led the Turkish Army to intervene, and on 8 March 1971 the government of Prime Minister Süleyman Demirel was forced to resign under pressure from General Cevdet Sunay as the Turkish military took control of the country, imposing martial law.

Three months later the president of Robert College, John Scott Everton, announced that the Board of Trustees had reached an agreement with the Ministry of Education in which it would take over the campus of Robert College, the collegiate division of which would become a Turkish institution, to be named Bosphorus University. At the same time, Robert Academy would be amalgamated with the American College for Girls in Arnavutköy as a co-educational secondary school under the name Robert College, administered by the American Board of Trustees.

The transition took place in the summer of 1971, and that September our campus began a new existence as Bosphorus University, whose first rector was my friend and colleague Aptullah Kuran, an alumnus of RC, a distinguished historian of Ottoman architecture and committed to perpetuating the bicultural Turkish–American tradition of the old Robert

College. Hilary's reaction to this transition is recorded in the minutes of the faculty meeting at which the changeover was announced: 'Robert College is dead, long live Robert College!'

Martial law was still in effect as we were working on *Strolling*, and a number of our left-wing students had been arrested and imprisoned, while others had gone into hiding. One of these, Cahit Düzel, had been living in a room in Hilary's basement. When the police raided the house they found what they claimed was 'Communist propaganda', which he had been distributing. Hilary was placed under house arrest and charged with harbouring a fugitive from justice. A detective was quartered in Cahit's room and listened to all of Hilary's telephone calls on an extension, breaking in on conversations to inform English-speaking callers that they must speak Turkish. When I called on Hilary in the evening to go over a chapter of *Strolling* we would be joined by the detective, a pleasant young man who listened attentively to our conversation, although he didn't know a word of English, and enjoyed the Hill Cocktails that Monik served to him whenever she brought us another round.

Many of our students and some of our Turkish colleagues were imprisoned in the Selimiye Barracks on the Asian side of the city, a huge structure that had served as Florence Nightingale's hospital during the Crimean War. Hilary, too, was confined there for a couple of days, during which time he was cleared of the charge against him and released from house arrest. The detective who had been living in the basement asked if he could stay, and Hilary said, 'Of course you can, my dear,' but the police authorities didn't permit him to do so.

After Hilary was cleared, he and I checked all the ancient Greek, Roman, Byzantine and Ottoman monuments we had described, revising our descriptions of those that had been restored or had deteriorated since we had last seen them. We noted in the introduction that these monuments were described in the context of the living city of which they had always been an integral part – sometimes built on, and from, the ruins of more ancient edifices that had preceded them on the same spot. Istanbul was a palimpsest, a canvas that had been painted and repainted over and over again, and we penetrated through the successive layers in writing our accounts, also describing the colourful life of the neighbourhoods in the historical peninsula. Most of that aspect of *Strolling* was my contribution, in which I quoted extensively from the *Seyyahatnâme* of Evliya Çelebi.

Once our survey was completed, we wrote the final draft of *Strolling*, and then, once Bill Edmonds had edited it, I helped him see it through the printers, who didn't know a word of English. The book was finally published in the late autumn of 1972, and I took the first two copies off the press to Hilary's apartment that evening. He was delighted, and we each took a copy and began to read through the book together as we sipped our cocktails.

At my suggestion we played a game in which whoever found a typographical error scored a point. We progressed rapidly, for though the book was more than 500 pages long, we knew it by heart, so it only took about three hours and half-a-dozen Hill Cocktails. The game ended in a tie, with each of us having found fifty typos. We agreed that the funniest error came in our description of Haghia Sophia, which we both believed to be the greatest building in the world, its massive dome still standing nearly fifteen centuries after it was erected. We had written that the arches supporting the dome 'rested on four huge piers', but the 'r' in the last word had been omitted, leaving the dome resting on four huge 'pies'.

I called up Bill Edmonds and had him correct that and the other errors before the full print run was started some days later, though inevitably other typos turned up. *Strolling* was distributed only in Istanbul, where it sold out, and copies made their way to the UK and US, receiving rave reviews, with *The Times* rating it as 'the best travel guide to Istanbul' and William Buckley in the *International Herald Tribune* describing it as 'a guide book that reads like a novel'.

Hilary passed away in 1976, just a few months after his retirement. He was laid to rest in the Protestant cemetery in the Feriköy quarter of Istanbul, his grave surrounded by those of many of his old colleagues at Robert College – all very different from one another, the one quality they shared being their love for the city in which they had lived out most of their adult lives.

We gathered around the raw grave, listening to the Anglican chaplain committing Hilary to the dust from which he had come a lifetime ago. We watched the earth receive Hilary and saw his casket disappear as a mound was shovelled over his grave. Then, in the dappled shade of a spectral cypress, his companion Michael Austin recited Gerard Manley Hopkins's poem 'Pied Beauty', Hilary's favourite.

> *Glory be to God for dappled things –*
> *For skies of couple-colour as a brinded cow;*
> *For rose-moles all in stipple upon trout that swim;*
> *Fresh-firecoal chestnut-falls; finch's wings;*
> *Landscape plotted and pieced – fold, fallow and plough;*
> *And all trades, their gear and tackle and trim.*
> *All things counter, original, spare, strange;*
> *Whatever is fickle, freckled (who knows how?)*
> *With swift, slow; sweet, sour; adazzle, dim;*
> *He fathers-forth whose beauty is past change: Praise him.*

Strolling Through Istanbul has been reprinted in new editions many times, most recently in 2010, when IB Tauris in London issued a completely revised and updated edition which I wrote for them because the city had changed so profoundly in the interim. But the core of *Strolling* remains the same, and as I browse through it I recall the lost city that I knew then. And when I find some of Hilary's phrases that have survived all the revisions, he seems to be speaking to me from beyond the grave, a Hill Cocktail in his hand.

AKŞAM

17

Amerikan filosu bu sabah gidiyor...

Adana'da 6. Filo aleyhine miting yapanları AP'liler dövdü

Taksim'de bekleyen grup, protesto mitingine katılanlara taş, bıçak ve sopalarla saldırdı

Taksim'de 30 bin kişi dövüştü 2 ölü var

Çatışma askeri birliklerin yardımı ile bastırıldı, 200 yaralı için radyo ile devamlı kan istendi

Prof. B.Nuri Esen dikkati çekti:

"Bir kuvvet müdahalesi yakındır,,

Prof. Kubalı: "Temel Hak tasarısı olağanüstü hal rejimi ihdas ediyor,,

25 kişi nezaret altına alındı

Bölükbaşı: "İktidarın Türk milletini aldatmasına müsaade etmiyeceğiz,,

Milli Ordu düzeni

CHAPTER 7

THE LEGLESS BEGGAR

W HEN I FIRST MET Michael Austin he was living with Hilary Sumner-Boyd while on vacation from Oxford, where he was completing his doctoral dissertation on the spoken Turkish of Istanbul. Mike was in his mid-twenties at the time, a tall and strikingly handsome Adonis, with a wicked wit and a very genuine charm that attracted both women and men – though in his own reckless passion for beautiful boys he sometimes came perilously close to the abyss.

Mike and I became very good friends, and I would often run into him in some of the more disreputable drinking places in the old Latin Quarter of Beyoğlu, where we would have a few beers together before he went off with one or another of the rather scary young men who hung out in those joints.

My favourite spot in Beyoğlu was the colourful Galatasaray fish market and the L-shaped alleyway known as Çiçek Pasajı, the Passage of Flowers, which connected it with the old Grand' Rue de Pera. The name of the alleyway came from the flower market which had once been located there, but had long since vanished, to be replaced by meyhanes, taverns famous for their draft beer served in giant glasses known as Argentines. The customers, all men, sat on high stools at long tables inside the meyhanes or outside in the alleyway itself, at slabs of marble laid on top of beer barrels.

One of the meyhanes had a tiny outside bar at which one or two customers could drink standing up, and one day I stopped there for an

Argentine. The bartender introduced himself as Abdurrahman, and though my Turkish was primitive we chatted away, finding out about one another's lives – the first of many such conversations I would have with Turks I met in the Çiçek Pasajı.

I met other foreigners there too, for the American and British Consulates and the English High School were close by. The British tended to go to a meyhane directly across the alley from the one where I hung out. They called it 'the Church', for on Sunday mornings the men drank there while their wives and children attended services at the Anglican chapel in the old British Embassy. I named my meyhane 'the Senate' because of the vociferous political discussions that were always going on there, particularly during our first months, for the government of Prime Minister Adnan Menderes had been overthrown in a military coup the previous May, and after a contentious trial he and two of his ministers were hanged later in the autumn.

One of those I met in the Pasaj was the Turkish poet Cevat Çapan, who was a regular at the Church. Cevat had graduated from Robert College and gone on to get a doctorate in Irish literature at Cambridge, where he founded the Irish–Turkish Poetry Society. I sometimes joined Cevat and his friends at the Church, where they met regularly at midday on Friday, having their first rakı at the time of the noon prayer, a ritual that continues to the present day.

I also got to know some of the beggars and musicians who passed through the Pasaj. One of them was a darkly handsome young man without legs who moved about on a home-made skateboard, going from one meyhane to another looking for handouts, always with dignity. I gave him a two-and-a-half-lira coin, and after thanking me he asked where I was from. I told him I was an American from New York. He smiled and said that if I went over to New York for a visit he would appreciate it if I would bring him back a pair of artificial legs. I said I would, and he thanked me again before rolling away to the next meyhane. He repeated this request whenever he stopped at my meyhane in the weeks that followed, and I always gave him the same answer. It became a ritual between us.

Early one Friday evening, as I was having a beer in my meyhane while waiting for Toots to finish shopping in the fish market, Mike Austin strolled by and joined me. While we were drinking, the legless beggar rolled up and greeted Mike with great affection, after which he took my coin and thanked me, before bidding us good evening and rolling away. I was surprised that he didn't go through our usual ritual and ask me to bring him a pair of artificial legs. But Mike smiled, saying, 'I suppose he's asked you to bring him back a pair of legs from the US?' When I said he had, Mike laughed. 'Well, don't bother,' he said. The bugger's got legs!' Then he told me the story.

The young man's name was Cem (pronounced Jem), and Mike had first met him in the Çiçek Pasajı a couple of years before and bought him a few drinks. Cem invited Mike back to his place, a ramshackle hut in the slums of Kasımpaşa, and there he excused himself for a few minutes to go and change. When Cem returned he was wearing a suit and standing as tall as Mike, walking nimbly on prosthetic limbs. They then went dancing in a gay club before returning to spend the night together in Cem's shack. Mike said that they had got together a few times after that, but after Mike had gone back up to Oxford they had lost contact – until this evening. 'You won't see Cem for a while,' Mike said. 'He'll do his begging elsewhere till he thinks you've left Istanbul, so that you won't give away his secret.' He was right. I didn't see Cem again for weeks, and when he reappeared and spotted me, he rolled by my meyhane without making eye contact. Abdurrahman, the barman, laughed, for he knew exactly what had been going on. This was part of the nightly theatre he had been watching for years in the Çiçek Pasajı.

Another evening I was due to meet Toots at Rejans, the Russian restaurant near the fish market, when I ran into Mike, who suggested we have a few beers in Lefter's, a Greek meyhane on Nevizade Sokak, near the Çiçek Pasajı. Lefter's was a hangout for Turkish writers, most notably Yaşar Kemal, who had several times been nominated for the Nobel Prize. The most notable of the characters there was a Greek alcoholic named Thanasi, whose speciality was dancing with an open rakı bottle balanced on his head, without spilling a drop, then drinking it all as appreciative customers flung money at him.

Thanasi also had an annoying habit of walking around the meyhane and helping himself to choice bits of food from the tables when he thought no one was looking. One evening Lefter stopped at our table and told us he was going to teach Thanasi a lesson. It seems they had killed a big rat, which the cook had roasted and prepared as if it were stifado, or roast rabbit – Thanasi's favourite dish – then dished up on a tray as though it was to be brought to one of the tables. When Thanasi saw what he thought was a dish of stifado he began picking away at it. As soon as he'd finished, Lefter told him he'd just eaten a rat, whereupon Thanasi threw up and then fainted. Thanasi was a changed man after that, at least to the extent that he no longer stole food from the tables at Lefter's.

After Mike received his doctorate from Oxford he joined the faculty of Robert College, teaching in the humanities program along with Hilary. He was given an apartment on the top floor of the old gatehouse at the lower end of the Twisty-Turny. Soon after he moved in, Toots and I were invited to a house-warming party, along with people from the College and some of Mike's Turkish friends from town, including one of the dangerous-looking young men I had noticed him with in Beyoğlu.

I didn't see Mike for a few weeks after that, for we were away on holiday. After we returned I called on Hilary one evening, and in the course of the conversation I asked him how Mike was doing. He hesitated before answering, looking distressed. Then he told me Mike had gone back to England for a while on sick leave. Finally, after another pause, he revealed that Mike had attempted to commit suicide after breaking up with his lover, apparently the young man I had seen him with in town and at his party. He had tried to hang himself from the chandelier in his apartment, but it broke under his weight and he fell to the floor. His downstairs neighbour heard the noise and went up to see what had happened. After getting the janitor to open the door, they found Mike lying on the floor unconscious. An ambulance was called and the medics managed to revive him before taking him off to the American Hospital.

Once the doctors had made sure that he had suffered no significant physical injury, he was moved to the psychiatric ward and kept under suicide watch. Hilary contacted Mike's family, who arranged for him to be transferred to a hospital in England, where he seemed to be recovering.

After a few years teaching in Beirut, Mike returned to Istanbul. He had put on a little weight and was a bit subdued at first, but before long he was his old self again, though I had the feeling that he was no longer as reckless as in the past.

After the Turkish Government took over the campus in 1971, I continued at Bosphorus University until 1976, when the Government reduced its funding and most of the foreign faculty were forced to leave. Toots and I moved to Athens, where for the next three years I taught at the Hellenic International School. It was the beginning of our seventeen-year exile from Istanbul.

Mike came to visit us soon after our arrival in Athens and told us that Hilary had just passed away. A few months later he wrote to say he had married Susan Hunter, a good friend of ours who had been teaching at the Robert College Community School. They had decided to leave Istanbul and move to Athens, for Mike was fluent in Greek and thought they could begin a new life there.

The Austins arrived a few months later and rented an apartment near ours in Kifissia, the old garden suburb of Athens at the foot of Mount Pendeli. We saw a great deal of one another in the months that followed, and I was glad to see they were enjoying their new life in Athens as much as we were. But one Saturday morning, when I met Michael for a drink at a café in Kifissia, I noticed that his eyes were red and bloodshot. I asked him what was wrong. He told me he hadn't slept the night before because he'd been weeping for Istanbul. And that almost set me to weeping too, for I missed our old life there as much as Mike did.

After we left Athens in 1979 we lost contact with the Austins for a while, though we received news of them occasionally from friends in Istanbul. I knew Mike had always wanted to be a man of the cloth, so I was very pleased when I learned he had been ordained as a priest in the Anglican Church. I was also pleased to hear he had been appointed chaplain of St Helena's, the chapel of the old British Embassy in Istanbul. The chapel was just a short walk from the Galatasaray Fish Market and the Çiçek Pasajı, and all the drinking places he and I used to frequent. I wondered if Mike was frequenting them again, for if so he might well run into Cem, the apparently legless beggar, or even the lowlife lover who had broken his heart.

After Athens, Toots and I spent eight years in the suburbs of Boston. I taught at the Noble and Greenough School for eight years before we burnt our bridges and moved to London, where I had found a job at Southbank International School. Maureen and her first husband, Paul Spike, were at the time living in Oxford with their two children, and it was through them that we once again linked up with the Austins. They had run into Mike in a village in the Cotswolds, where he was pastor of the local church. Apparently he and Susan were quite happy with their new life, which couldn't have been more different from our old bohemian existence in Istanbul.

Toots and I spent the Christmas vacation in Oxford with Maureen and Paul and our grandchildren Matthew and Emma. The day before Christmas we drove to the Cotswolds village where the Austins were living – without telling them, for I wanted to surprise Mike, whom I hadn't seen in more than eight years. We checked the time for the Christmas Eve service at Mike's church and arrived early so we could get good seats. We were among the first, seating ourselves towards the front of the nave on the left, where I took the seat at the end of the pew on the aisle. I looked around and saw Susan sitting in the front pew on the left, talking to an elderly couple so intently that she didn't notice us.

The organist started playing and a bell tinkled as a double line of altar boys emerged from the sacristy with lighted candles, followed by Mike, resplendent in his ecclesiastical robes. He was the perfect priest, and as he conducted the service I could see that he was born for the role. But I still wondered how he dealt with the loss of his beloved Istanbul.

When the service ended, the altar boys walked in procession down the nave, with Mike behind them, blessing his parishioners to left and right. When he reached our pew he was blessing those on the other side, so I reached out and put my hand on his arm. He turned in some puzzlement and was so surprised to see me that he shouted in Turkish, '*Eşşoğuleşek!*', meaning 'son of a donkey', and it took a moment before he regained his composure and continued down the aisle. While the congregation craned their necks to see what had brought on this astonishing outburst, I tried to keep a bland expression on my face, hoping none of the parishioners understood Turkish.

Outside, we waited until Mike had finished talking with his parishioners, and then he walked over, embracing us one by one. When my turn came he said, 'You old bugger, you!' and we laughed together with tears in our eyes.

By that time Susan had joined as, and after we had embraced one another she introduced us to the couple with whom she had been conversing in the church. Mike changed his clothes in the sacristy and then led us all to the local pub, where I could tell that he was well known and very popular. He and I talked for a bit, laughing as we recalled some of our escapades in Istanbul.

While he went on to talk to the rest of the family I began chatting with the gentleman to whom Susan had introduced us outside the church. He turned out to be a very interesting character, and I could see why he and his wife were such good friends of the Austins. I asked him how Mike was doing and he said the parishioners really liked him, though he was very different from all his predecessors. Then he laughed and said that Mike was a bit too close to the altar boys, and had better watch his step. When I said goodbye to Mike I had the feeling that I would never see him again. From the look in his eyes I could see that he felt that way too.

We had no word of the Austins until we finally returned to Istanbul in 1993 At our first get-together with old friends we learned that Mike had passed away the previous year. He was buried in the graveyard of the church in the Cotswolds where we had last seen him, and Susan was still living in the village.

On the first Saturday of the semester I took a late-afternoon stroll through the Çiçek Pasajı, the first time I had been there in seventeen years. I was shocked by how much had changed, for all the meyhanes had been transformed into respectable restaurants, with beggars and street musicians no longer allowed entrance. The Pasaj had lost all the rough edges that gave it its anarchic character.

The little outside bar where Abdurrahman used to serve me Argentines was no longer there, so I sat down at an outside table of the meyhane across the passageway, the one the Brits used to call the Church. I looked inside and saw an old friend, the Turkish poet Cevat Çapan, sitting with his cronies, drinking rakı.

Cevat came out to join me, welcoming me back to Istanbul. He asked if I had any news of Mike Austin, who had been a good friend of his. I told him Mike had passed away, and we sat there in silence for a while. Then we began reminiscing about Mike and his escapades, particularly those set in the Çiçek Pasajı. Cevat laughed and said, 'I remember seeing the two of you standing at Abdurrahman's bar one evening, talking to that legless beggar. I think his name was Cem. He's probably gone too, like everyone else we knew then.'

We sat there in silence again, and as dusk gathered around us I felt the presence of those I had known here half a lifetime ago, all of them passing in procession through the Passage of Flowers, just as I had reviewed them standing with Mike at Abdurrahman's bar.

Opposite: The old Çiçek Pasajı, or Flower Passage, a favourite haunt

CHAPTER 8

THE IMAGINARY DOG

CHARLES ADELSEN AND Henry Angelo Castillon first came to
Istanbul in 1960, the same year we did, but though we were
aware of their presence from the articles they published in
various newspapers and magazines, we didn't meet them until
a couple of years later. Many of their early articles were travel pieces about
historical sites in Turkey, for which Charles wrote the text and Henry took
the photographs. Mass tourism had not yet discovered Turkey at that time,
and their articles, particularly those about more remote sites, were often the
first-ever descriptions of places which later became internationally famous.

I first met Charles and Henry when they came to Rumelihisarı to
interview James Baldwin for an article for *Ebony* magazine. At the time
Jimmy was living in the Pasha's Library, an Ottoman building just outside
the College campus, and I ran into them at a friend's house later that day.
It was the beginning of a lifelong friendship.

Charles and Henry were an odd couple in every sense of the phrase,
for they were oddly matched and each of them was odd in quite different
ways. There were very few foreigners living in Istanbul at the time, so we
usually got to know one another very well, particularly those of us living
in self-imposed exile, trying to escape the soul-killing uniformity of the
modern world.

Charles and Henry were secretive about their age, but eventually
I learned that they were both born in 1927, which made them a year
younger than me. Charles was American and Henry from Peru, where his

great-grand-uncle had been Archbishop of Lima, so he claimed. Henry had acquired US citizenship after moving to Los Angeles, where he had met Charles. Once, after a few drinks, Charles told me they had met at a gay bar in LA, where Henry's first attempts to pick him up were so aggressive that Charles threatened to call the police. But before the evening was over they had become a couple.

Charles had been a child actor in Hollywood and had gone to the same school as Shirley Temple. But he never rose above bit parts, his biggest role in the 1938 film *Marie Antoinette*, starring Norma Shearer and Tyrone Power, in which Charles played one of the pageboys at the French court. Like most child actors in Hollywood, Charles never graduated to adult roles, so when he came of age he shifted to a career in journalism. After he met Henry, a professional photographer, they began their careers as photojournalists, moving to Turkey because it was still terra incognita, waiting to be discovered.

Besides Charles and Henry, there were three other gay men in our extended social circle – George Bacon, Dan Parrish and Dimitri Nesteroff – whose own eccentric circles revolved tangentially around ours. All were self-imposed exiles, originals who simply didn't fit into conventional modern life, truly 'odd men out'.

George Bacon had also been a child actor in Hollywood, and he too had failed to find roles as an adult. His one big chance had come when he tried out for one of the leading parts in the 1937 screen version of *Captains Courageous*, based on the novel by Rudyard Kipling, which was nominated for four Academy Awards and for which Spencer Tracy won Best Actor. George had auditioned for the part that would eventually go to Freddie Bartholomew, who had already starred in five films and became Hollywood's highest-paid child star after Shirley Temple.

George's full name was George Vaux Bacon. Reading a book about the silent-movie era recently, I discovered that there was an actor named George Vaux Bacon who starred in American films prior to the First World War. A photo of him with Pearl White, star of *The Perils of Pauline*, showed a strong resemblance to the George Bacon I knew, which made me wonder if he was George's father.

I also found a series of newspaper articles, including one from *The New York Times*, about a George Vaux Bacon convicted of being a German spy during the First World War. It seems that Bacon, an actor and drama critic, was recruited by Albert Sander, a German agent in New York, and sent to England to spy on British military installations. He was arrested by Scotland Yard, convicted of espionage and sentenced to death. But when he revealed everything he knew about the German network, he was handed over to the American authorities and taken back to be tried in the New York District Court. There, after pleading guilty, he was sentenced by Judge Van Fleet to a year and a day in a federal penitentiary. A *Times* article dated 28 March 1917 reads:

> BACON GETS YEAR AND DAY IN PRISON.
> American Spy, Sentenced to Death in England,
> Pleads Guilty Here.
> SAYS HE BLUFFED GERMANS. Had Always Wanted to Go
> to Europe, He Tells Judge, and so Hired Himself to Sander.
>
> George Vaux Bacon, the American citizen who hired himself
> as a spy to Albert Sander, the German agent in this country,
> pleaded guilty in Federal District Court yesterday and
> was sentenced by Judge Van Fleet to serve a year and a day
> in the Federal Penitentiary in Atlanta, Georgia. He says,
> 'I bluffed the Germans as long as I could and remained
> abroad. While in England I was tried and convicted of being
> a spy. I really think that I was only guilty of procuring
> money from the Germans by false pretences.'

Judge Van Fleet – saying he disliked very much to send such a bright young man to penitentiary, although he had pleaded guilty to a grave offence, which was more political than penal – then sentenced him. He stated that he hoped the sentence would be a deterrent to other plotters.

I found Bacon's penitentiary mugshots, front and side views, and could see a definite resemblance to George, even more pronounced than in the photo with Pearl White. So I am reasonably sure that this was George's father – not only because of the facial resemblance, but also his offbeat flair for the dramatic, which was quintessentially George Bacon. Bacon served his sentence and, in 1920, received a pardon from President Woodrow Wilson.

The same George Vaux Bacon appears to have been one of the Surrealist New York Dada poets. I came across several volumes of his poems, written between 1913 and 1937, the year that the George I knew unsuccessfully auditioned for *Captains Courageous*. After that the trail grows cold, for both George Vaux Bacons, father and son. So far as I know, there is no further record of the name until the early 1960s, when the George Vaux Bacon I knew turned up in Istanbul. But George, like all of the other 'odd men out' that I knew, never spoke about his father.

Charles, on the other hand, did occasionally speak of his step-father, an eccentric multimillionaire whose portrait he once showed us, dressed in the uniform of a Japanese commodore. There was also a youthful photo of his mother, who bore a striking resemblance to the actress Bette Davis. In one of the best examples of name-dropping I ever heard, Charles told us he had once been having lunch with his mother in a studio cafeteria in Hollywood when Peter Lorre tried to pick her up, until their mutual friend Boris Karloff stopped by and led him away.

Dan Parrish never spoke of either his mother or his father, and nor did Dimitri Nesteroff. When we first met them, Dan was teaching in the English Language Preparatory Division of Robert Academy, while Dimitri was a Reuters stringer. Both were men of self-created mystery, and the stories they told of their pre-Istanbul lives were different at every telling, though with enough truth at the core that I was able to piece together their backgrounds.

Dan was from Texas, as I guessed from his accent and some of the framed photographs in his apartment, one of which showed him in a cowboy outfit, wearing a Stetson, with the flag of the Lone Star State behind him on the wall. But that could have been just a stage setting, for Dan was always acting, on stage or off, directing those around him in the drama that he created around his everyday life.

Dimitri had been born in London of Russian émigré parents, or so he said, and I could well believe it from his accent as well as his appearance and persona, for he was Russian to the core. He claimed to have served in the British Army during the Second World War, which may very well have been true, but his anecdotes of fighting against the Japanese in Burma in the summer of 1945 were certainly not. I had been in Burma at that time with a US Navy commando unit, and could tell that his war stories were pure fantasy. But they were entertaining nonetheless, so I never bothered to contradict him.

Charles and Henry had no sources of income other than what they earned from their articles, so they were careful with their money, counting on friends like ourselves to invite them to dinner. And they had no shortage of invitations, for they were very entertaining guests. Charles would play the piano for hours on end, his repertoire including classical music, ragtime, jazz, popular songs and even national anthems, while Henry played the Spanish guitar and danced flamenco. They repaid these dinner invitations by taking us and their other hosts with them to the national-day celebrations of all the countries with consulates in Istanbul, gathering up leftover canapés to bring home with them as they left.

Charles and Henry occasionally invited us to their tiny apartment for supper, where fellow guests ranged from Bulgarian wrestlers to Turkish and Kurdish taxi drivers, and the food was usually leftover canapés from the last consular reception we had attended together. They had a young Albanian refugee named Tarık working for them as a live-in houseboy, and he was able to keep the wrestlers and taxi drivers in check, at least while Toots and I were there. I could see that Tarık was genuinely fond of Charles and Henry, and he remained with them as their faithful companion for the rest of their days.

Maureen was due to graduate from Harvard in June 1974, so I arranged for my final exams to be given early so that Toots and I could attend the graduation. A few weeks before we left Istanbul, I received a letter from Stonehouse Press, a New York publishing house, asking if I was interested in writing a book about Istanbul. I replied saying that I was, and made an appointment to see the commissioning editor, Helene Jordan, in New York on our way to Maureen's graduation.

The book, Helene told me, was to be called *Next Stop Istanbul*, one in a series of profusely illustrated guides to the great cities of the world. She offered me a fee of $1,000, which was very little, but I accepted immediately because we were flat broke, and, besides, it wouldn't take much time – I could simply recycle information from my other books on the city. When Helene asked if I could recommend a professional photographer to take the colour photos for the book, I put her in touch with Henry, who quickly came to an agreement with her – at a significantly higher fee than mine, since there would be much more work involved, or so he claimed.

Once we had returned to Istanbul I checked in with Henry and Charles, and together we drew up an outline of the book. Henry already had a vast collection of colour photos of Istanbul, so we made a selection for *Next Stop Istanbul* and then walked around the city so he could take new photographs of recently restored monuments. But when it came to making a final selection, I realised we had no interior photos of any of the picturesque old *yalıs*, the seaside mansions along the Bosphorus. The most historic and beautiful of these were along the shores of the Sweet Waters of Asia, directly across the Bosphorus from Rumelihisarı. I knew some of the old Ottoman aristocrats who lived there, and we decided to try to gain entry to one their *yalıs*.

The owner of the Ostrorog Yalı was Count Jean Ostrorog, whose family had lived there for more than two centuries. Polish-French aristocrats, they had first established links with the Ottoman Empire in the late eighteenth century. I called the Count and told him about our book and, knowing he was interested in Hollywood films, mentioned that Charles was a contemporary of Shirley Temple. He was very excited and invited us to a lawn party he was giving in his *yalı* the following Sunday afternoon for all his old friends in the Sweet Waters. He looked forward to seeing us there around noon, he said.

The following Sunday, Toots and I met Charles and Henry at the ferry station in Rumelihisarı, where we hired a boatman to row us across. Approaching the Ostrorog Yalı I could see the Count and his guests clustered around the landing, looking expectantly in our direction. But when we landed they all seemed somewhat disappointed. After the Count had welcomed us and introduced us to his guests, he told me privately that he had thought I was bringing Shirley Temple to the party. I apologised for the misunderstanding, but he laughed and said it didn't matter, for Charles and Henry were very charming.

While Charles supervised Henry's photography of the *yalı's* interior, the Count sat Toots down with his wife and some of her women friends. He then introduced me to a very charming old gentleman named Ahmet Bey, with whom I spent the rest of the afternoon, listening to fascinating tales of his service as an officer in the Ottoman Army in Palestine during the First World War, including his friendship with Colonel Newcombe, an associate of Lawrence of Arabia. It was a most memorable afternoon, particularly because it was the very last time we were privileged to attend a gathering of the old Ottoman aristocracy along the Sweet Waters of Asia. Within a few years their unique world had come to an end, and we ourselves had begun our long exile from the Bosphorus.

We kept in contact with Charles and Henry during our seventeen-year absence from Istanbul, and while we were living in the Boston area they came to see us. They had left Tarık behind to look after their apartment and belongings and were renting a small place in Springfield, Massachusetts, where Charles's mother was in a very expensive nursing home. Charles told us he was trying to get his mother out of the home and bring her to Istanbul, for the bills were eating up the estate he hoped to inherit. Meanwhile, the doctor who owned the nursing home had persuaded his mother to give him control of her estate, and so Charles had come to get it back.

I put Charles in touch with a lawyer in Boston who enabled him to regain control of his mother's estate, which, as I learned, amounted to about $20 million. The next step was to get her out of the nursing home and back to Istanbul. This took some time, for Charles first had to find a much larger apartment in Istanbul, since he needed extra rooms for his mother and a live-in nurse, not to mention her family heirlooms.

That left the problem of how to fly his mother back to Istanbul, which was complicated by the fact that she had to be accompanied. I volunteered to help, for the Turkish Ministry of Culture, in appreciation of the many books I had written about Turkey, had given me two round-trip business-class tickets to Istanbul on THY, Turkey's national airline. So at the beginning of the summer vacation Toots and I booked seats on the same flight as Charles's mother, who was coming in an ambulance from the nursing home to the airport in Boston.

Toots and I were already seated when she was brought aboard in a wheelchair, raising a huge fuss which attracted attention of everyone on the plane. I told one of the hostesses that Toots and I were accompanying the woman who had just been wheeled aboard and asked her what the problem was. She looked at me in some puzzlement, telling me that two seats had been booked for Charles's mother, and she assumed the other seat was for the person who was to accompany her. She looked even more puzzled when I explained, with some difficulty, that two seats had been reserved for Charles's mother because one of them was for her, the other for her imaginary dog, and that Toots and I would look after both of them. The hostess finally believed me when I greeted Charles's mother and patted her imaginary dog, which quieted her down, though all the other passengers in business class must have thought that I was stark raving mad.

Charles was waiting at the airport in Istanbul with a nurse and an ambulance, and they took his mother to the new apartment he and Henry had rented. Toots and I visited them there several times before we flew back to Boston at the end of the summer, and everything appeared to be going well. Charles's mother seemed happy, smiling as she patted her imaginary dog, though Charles himself seemed to be losing his patience with her, and told me privately that she was driving him mad.

By the time we next returned to Istanbul, in 1988, Charles's mother had passed away. Charles had taken her remains back to the US to be buried in Hollywood, he told us, for that was where she had been happiest. Then, with tears in his eyes, he said, 'You know, she pretended to have an imaginary dog even when I was a boy.'

By that time both George Bacon and Dimitri Nesteroff had also passed away, and Dan Parrish died soon afterwards, so Charles and Henry were the last of our 'odd men out', still clinging to the wreckage in our broken-down paradise. And then they too passed away, Henry in 1992 and Charles the following year. Charles had tried to keep his composure during

Henry's funeral at the church of St Esprit. But at the end of the requiem mass an orchestra of five violinists, including our grandchildren Ariadne and Alex, played Henry's favourite song, 'Danny Boy', which reduced him and everyone else to tears.

Charles's requiem mass took place at St Esprit the following year. Afterwards, we all proceeded to the Catholic cemetery in Feriköy and stood there together in the pouring rain, looking on in silence while Charles was laid to rest beside Henry. Their two tombstones stood there side by side, slightly akimbo, an odd couple even in the grave, the shades of our last 'odd men out' now haunting our lost city, along with those of George Bacon, Dimitri Nesteroff and Dan Parrish.

CHAPTER 9

BURIAL OF A BOHEMIAN

JIMMY BALDWIN WAS NOT the only uninvited guest at our first party. Shortly after his arrival, our dear friend Minnie Garwood showed up with an old school friend of hers, whom she introduced simply as Magali, who had just returned to Istanbul after years in the US. Magali looked sad and dispirited at first, but after a few drinks she began dancing with Jimmy Baldwin, the two of them swearing at one another in French and breaking up with laughter as they exchanged insults. While they were wheeling around the floor, Minnie told me a bit about Magali, whom she had known since they attended Notre Dame de Sion, the French girls' school in Istanbul.

Magali was the same age as Minnie and me, all three of us born in 1926 – Minnie in Istanbul, me in Brooklyn and Magali in Paris. Magali was a Giraud, a French family who had originally come to Istanbul in 1536, when Francis I established diplomatic and trade relations with Süleyman the Magnificent.

Her family had spent summer vacations in Polonezköy, a Polish village founded in 1848 on the Asian side of the Upper Bosphorus, and Magali had her first big romance there, with a young Polish potato farmer who wanted to marry her. But when she was eighteen she went off to Beirut and tried to join the Free French Army. When they turned her down she found a job as a typist working for the OSS, the US intelligence service. There she married an American officer named Miller, and after the war went back with him to live in the US. They had two daughters, Terry and Jeannie.

The marriage broke up after a couple of years, and Magali next married a truck driver, Morgan, by whom she had a son, Larry. By Larry's account his father was a 'gambler and wannabe cowboy', whose ashes he would scatter over the Grand Canyon. But that marriage eventually broke up too, and on the rebound Magali married another gambler named Gaster, whom she divorced after a couple of years. She returned to Istanbul with her children, hoping to make a fresh start, and that was when fate delivered her to our door – intertwining her life inexorably with ours.

Later that autumn Magali went to stay with the Whittalls, Levantine relatives of hers, at their estate in Moda, on the Asian side of the Lower Bosphorus. One day, while the Whittalls were having a party, Magali took a walk in their gardens and fell into an overgrown cistern. She found herself lying next to an old drunkard who thought that she must be an angel, fallen from heaven. Magali's screams alerted the Whittalls, who came and lifted her out. They carried her back to the house and called a doctor, who found that she had broken both legs in several places.

Magali recuperated for several weeks at the Whittalls, and once she could hobble about on crutches they helped her back to her mother's house in Bebek. It was there, a month or so later, that she met Hilmar Gottesthal, an Austrian painter and sculptor about fifteen years her junior, who became the love of Magali's life – as I could tell when I first saw them together.

Once Magali had fully recovered, she found a job in the English Language Preparatory Division of Robert College, but soon resigned, finding that the restrictions of regular employment and the need to keep up a respectable front were not for her – unconventional bohemian that she was – particularly after she and Hilmar began living together. She decided to concentrate on promoting and selling his paintings and sculptures, keeping house for him in a series of broken-down shacks which Hilmar transformed into works of art, each more original than the last.

The first of their dwellings was an abandoned, half-ruined Ottoman house in Rumelihisarı, where they moved in literally as squatters. Hilmar repaired the place so that it was not only liveable in but very attractive, particularly thanks to the odd bits and pieces with which Magali furnished it, some hand-me-downs from friends, others picked up in the flea market.

In those years some of us at the College, over a long weekend, would drive across the border to the lively Greek port town of Alexandropolis, where we always spent a couple of evenings at a tavern run by our friend Dimitri Drakakis, who had been born in Istanbul and had joint Greek and Turkish nationality. Magali and Hilmar joined Toots and me several times on these weekend jaunts, going in our old third-hand car, an Opel, which I christened 'Opeless' because it was in such desperately bad repair.

After Magali and Hilmar had moved into the house in Rumelihisarı, they invited Dimitri to come and stay with them, and he accepted with pleasure, agreeing to come as soon as he could arrange for one of his relatives to look after the tavern in his absence.

A few weeks later, teaching a physics class late on a Friday afternoon, I noticed a Greek taxi pull up on the roundabout across the campus from Albert Long Hall, where I was lecturing. The driver spoke to the watchman, who pointed to my lecture room. Dimitri then emerged from the taxi and, as I watched in astonishment, I saw him and the driver unload a barrel of wine from the taxi's boot and start rolling it across the campus to Albert Long Hall. I managed to intercept them, and after directing Dimitri to the house where Magali and Hilmar were living I went back to my students, who had witnessed the whole scene and were highly amused.

When the class was over I called Toots and told her of Dimitri's arrival. She prepared an early supper for the children and then she and I walked over to Magali's place, where we found an impromptu party well under way, with Dimitri and Magali singing together in Greek. The song was 'Yialo Yialo', which I knew well, so when they finished I sang the refrain, but in English rather than Greek.

> *If the sea were only wine*
> *And the mountains mezedhes,*
> *The ships could be the glasses*
> *For revellers to drink!*

The house in Rumelihisarı was eventually demolished to make way for a new building, and Magali and Hilmar moved to Kuruçeşme, a village farther down the Bosphorus, where they rebuilt and refurbished an abandoned workman's cottage on the hill high above the strait. They invited us to a housewarming as soon as they were settled in, and I could see they had worked their usual magic, for the little cottage had been transformed into a dream house, adorned with Hilmar's paintings and sculptures, the latter in marble and olive wood, some of them doubling as furniture.

Around this time Magali's son Larry, who had just turned sixteen went missing. She figured he had gone off with the gypsies he had been hanging round with on the Asian side of the Bosphorus, for he had inherited her bohemian ways. For two years she heard nothing of him, until he eventually wrote to her from Afghanistan, saying he was in a desperate condition and wanted to come home. She sent him the money he needed and he returned to Istanbul. Once he had settled in, Magali invited us all to a party to welcome him home.

A year later Larry surprised everyone by announcing that he was going to marry Jane King, a teacher at the Robert College Secondary School in Arnavutköy. Jane was in her late twenties, while Larry had just turned nineteen. Magali took it in her stride, remembering her own early marriage, and invited us all to the cottage in Kuruçeşme to celebrate the wedding.

Magali prevailed on the old Russian balalaika orchestra to come out of retirement and play at the ceremony, which was held on the terrace in front of the cottage. It was a beautiful day in early June, and as the balalaika orchestra played away I saw a school of dolphins gambolling in the Bosphorus below, pausing in their passage up the strait as if enchanted by the music. It was clearly a most favourable omen for the marriage – or so I thought at the time.

Shortly after the wedding we went off to spend the summer in Naxos, as we always did in those years. Not long after we'd arrived I took a walk along the beach outside the town, and to my great surprise ran into Larry, who appeared to be stoned. He said he and Jane had decided to spend their honeymoon there, living in a tiny house they had rented farther along the beach. I continued walking with him till we came to the house, which turned out to be just a windowless concrete block. Larry invited me in, and I was surprised to find Jane there with Şarl Shahbaz, whom I had last seen in

Aliye's apartment in Istanbul. They both seemed to be stoned too, and from the three sleeping bags on the floor I guessed they had formed a *ménage à trois*. After a strained attempt at conversation I left them to themselves.

Not long after, I learned that Larry was the odd man out. He left Jane with Şarl, and that effectively ended their marriage. I wasn't to see Larry again until several years had passed, by which time he was happily remarried and doing well as a film-maker.

Magali and Hilmar, meanwhile, continued to live in the cottage in Kuruçeşme. But when eventually that too was demolished to make way for a new building, they moved in with us – with all the children away at school, we had room to spare. They were ideal guests, though every now and then Magali would have one rakı too many in the evening and this would send her round the bend, swearing in English, Turkish, Greek and Polish, until Hilmar gave me a nod, after which we would immobilise her and carry her up to bed, where she usually fell sound asleep. The next morning she would reappear with no apparent memory of her behaviour.

By that time our old Opel was on its last legs and we decided to buy a new car. We gave Opeless to Magali and Hilmar, who repaired it enough to give it renewed life and took out the back seats so they could carry Hilmar's paintings and sculptures. For they had decided to start a new life in Greece.

Eventually they found themselves a place to live in Stomion, a seaside village in Thessaly, which Magali called 'Polonezköy on the Sea'. We visited them there a few years later to find they had worked their magic yet again, converting an abandoned fisherman's shack into a very original house and studio. They now owned a second-hand camper van, and over drinks on our first evening they told us of the last days of our old Opel.

After setting up house in Stomion they had driven off to see Magali's daughter Terry, who had married and was living in Scotland. They spent a week with her and her family then stopped off for a few days in London, staying at a cheap bed-and-breakfast place. On their first day there they decided they would drive to Buckingham Palace in order to present one of Hilmar's paintings to the Queen. I laughed when Magali told us this, for at first I thought she was joking. But the expression on her face told me she was deadly serious.

They had tried to enter the Palace, they told us, but were stopped by the police. Magali showed them the painting they wanted to present to the Queen and were told that it must be properly wrapped. So they set off to a stationery shop to buy paper, and then drove the parcelled-up painting back to the Palace. The police guard told them it would be delivered to the Queen, who subsequently sent Hilmar a gracious note of thanks, which they showed us that evening.

Magali and Hilmar drove on to Paris, and there the Opel finally met its end. Its motor beyond repair, it had to be towed to a junk yard, after which they had bought the camper and driven back to Stomion. That evening we drank a last toast to the Opeless of fond memory.

Eventually Magali and Hilmar decided to leave Stomion, for mass tourism had discovered the village, destroying its tranquillity and driving up prices so much that they could no longer afford to live there. Deciding to return to Turkey, they loaded all Hilmar's works of art into the camper and a trailer – along with their donkey, Greta Garbo. But when they reached the border the Turkish customs officials wouldn't let them bring Greta Garbo into the country – they already had more than enough donkeys in Turkey, they said. So Magali and Hilmar said goodbye to Greta, and the customs officials assured them they would keep her as a pet and take good care of her.

Magali and Hilmar eventually found what they wanted in Çınarcık, a village in the hills above the eastern shore of the Sea of Marmara, a few hours' drive south of Istanbul. Once again they restored a used shack in their own inimitable way, creating what I dubbed 'Polonezköy on the Marmara'. Indeed, on one of our many visits there we met three former mayors of Polonezköy, all of whom commented on how much Çınarcık resembled their own village, where Magali had spent her holidays as a child.

Çınarcık took its name from the many *çınars*, or plane trees, growing there, some of them hundreds of years old. When one of these venerable trees collapsed in a winter storm not long after their arrival, Hilmar had it dragged to the village square. There he stripped off the branches, raised its top a few feet above the ground, and hollowed out its trunk, creating a work of art that was also a tunnel, down which the village children could slide in a playground he created for them. When Magali brought this work to the attention of President Turgut Özal, he had it declared a national monument. I felt it was Magali and Hilmar themselves who together should have been declared a national monument – of both Turkey and Greece – for wherever they lived they turned their home and its surroundings into an original work of art in keeping with the character of its surroundings.

The last time I saw Magali and Hilmar together was in 1993, when Toots and I were living on the Lido in Venice. They had left Turkey and were on their way to Hilmar's birthplace in Austria, where they were to be married on what would be Magali's sixty-seventh birthday. They had shipped all of Hilmar's artworks to the US, for they planned to settle down in Flintstone, Maryland, where Magali's daughter Jeannie and her husband owned a large farm. Hilmar had built an old-fashioned log cabin beside a stream running through the farm, and they hoped to spend the rest of their days there, in what I called 'Polonezköy West'.

We only spent an hour or so together that day in Venice, since they were just there to transfer from the car ferry that had brought them from Izmir in Turkey to one bound for Trieste. We spent the time enjoying a little picnic in their van, and before we parted Magali gave us a leg from a wild boar which Hilmar had shot in the hills above Çınarcık before they left.

We waved to them as their ferry sailed away, then took the vaporetto back to the Lido. While Toots stopped for groceries at the supermarket on the Gran Viale, I waited on one of the benches outside. I soon found myself surrounded by dogs, straining at their leaches as they sniffed the boar meat I was carrying in a plastic bag. I laughed to myself, imagining what Magali would say when I told her about this the next time we were together.

But as fate would have it, we would never see Magali again. Five years later Toots and I were living in Manhattan for a few months. I had been commissioned to write a history of Robert College and was going through the archives in the New York office of the Near East Colleges Association. Our dear friends Roddy and Olga O'Connor spent a few days with us there, reminiscing about the good times we had spent together in Istanbul, where we had first met in 1961 at the one and only party that Magali threw during the brief period when she was teaching at Robert College.

The O'Connors had been in touch with Magali and Hilmar and knew their telephone number in Flintstone, so I suggested we call them. They were very pleased and surprised to hear from me and Toots, for we had not spoken since the day we parted company in Venice. We talked together for at least half an hour, until Magali finally said goodbye, in what I thought was a sad tone of voice.

I learned why a few months later, by which time Toots and I had returned to Istanbul. I received a letter from Hilmar telling me that Magali had just died of leukaemia. He said she had asked to be cremated, and for her ashes to be buried in Polonezköy, and that he was now arranging this. He would be in touch again when everything was organised.

A couple of months later Hilmar called to tell me all the arrangements for Magali's funeral were in place, and that he would be arriving at Atatürk Airport in two weeks' time. Magali's funeral was to be held in Polonezköy the Saturday after we arrived, and he asked me to invite all her old friends.

And so on the appointed day about fifty of us assembled in Polonezköy: old friends of Magali's from Robert College, people from the village, and relatives, including Larry Morgan. After a requiem mass in the village church we all walked to the cemetery, where we assembled around an open grave, at the head of which was a beautiful marble tombstone made for Magali by Hilmar. The village priest was standing there, and as Magali's funerary urn was placed in the grave and covered with earth he recited a last blessing in Polish. Then he and three old men, contemporaries of Magali, sang a Polish hymn, joined by all the villagers who had come to the cemetery.

At a Polish tavern in the village square, all the College people sat at one long table, with Hilmar at one end and Larry at the other. Hilmar stood and offered a toast to Magali's memory, saying she would have wanted all of us to enjoy ourselves at her last party. As the wine began flowing and the party was well under way, a sudden wind rustled the leaves of the trees embowering the village square. We were all silent for a moment. 'It's Magali!' I said. For I sensed it was her bohemian spirit, borne by the wind on her last journey. And so we drank to her again in farewell.

CHAPTER 10

THE ELEPHANT'S GRAVE

Afternoon returning from home leave in the US during the summer of 1963, Toots and I decided to try and find a place closer to the College. I began looking around, and on the first Saturday of the fall term I walked up from the Bosphorus along the cobbled road that passes the Aşiyan cemetery. There were only two houses on the side of the road opposite the cemetery, almost hidden away by the trees that cover the steep hillside below the College.

The lower house was obviously occupied, for there was a car in its driveway, but the upper one seemed to be empty. The only approach was off the side road leading up to the house (now a museum) of Tevfik Fikret, the poet who founded the Turkish Department at Robert College. About halfway up the road to his house, which he had called Aşiyan, or The Nest, I came to an iron gateway wrapped in a coil of barbed wire, with the name Nigâr carved on its lintel.

I walked through the gateway to see an old wooden Ottoman *köşk*, or villa, of three stories, with an octagonal gazebo on its uppermost level. A balcony projected from its *piano nobile* over an oval pool filled with tropical fish, surrounded by palmetto trees and a beautiful garden, at the back of which an immensely tall cypress was encircled by a stone seat so as to form a little round terrace looking out over the Bosphorus.

I made enquiries and found that the owner's name was Salih Nigâr, whom I had met at a College reception. He had mentioned that his father, Feridun, was one of the founding members of our Turkish Department, a colleague of Tevfik Fikret. So I called Salih Bey to ask if the house was for rent, and when he said it was we agreed to meet there in an hour's time.

Salih was waiting for me when I arrived and showed me round the house, which had been built in 1880 by his grandmother, the famous poet Nigâr Hanım. When she died in 1918 the *köşk* had passed to his father, who had lived there until a few years before his death, abandoning it after an angel appeared to him in a dream to warn him that the house was unlucky. Salih said the house had been unoccupied since then and he would be happy to rent it to me for the same amount the College was paying for our apartment in the Arifî Paşa Korusu.

So at the beginning of October we moved to Nigâr Hanım's Köşk. Meanwhile, in the College library I had found an English translation of a collection of the poems of Nigâr Hanım, a major figure in late Ottoman poetry. One of them, 'Tell Me Again', particularly impressed me, and when I read it to Toots that evening she felt it lent added romance to our move into the house where it had been written.

> *Am I your only love – in the whole world – now?*
> *Am I really the only object of your love?*
> *If passions rage in your mind,*
> *If love springs eternal in your heart –*
> *Is it all meant for me? Tell me again.*
>
> *Tell me right now, am I the only one who inspires*
> *All your dark thoughts, all your sadness?*
> *Share with me what you feel, what you think.*
> *Come, my love, pour into my heart*
> *Whatever gives you so much pain. Tell me again.*

When we took over the house, there was an Armenian family living on the ground floor, whom Salih Bey had asked me to keep on as caretakers. There was Mary Bardakcıyan – her actual name was Vartui – who agreed to work as our housekeeper, her husband, Avadis, their children, Artin and Ayda, along with Mary's brother, Haçik, and her mother, Nevart. Hagop and Kirkor were fishermen, but their full-time occupation seemed to be drinking. Together they outnumbered us six to five, which led my friend John Little to refer to our household as 'The Freely Plantation'.

It took us a couple of weeks to make ourselves at home at Nigâr Hanım's Köşk, and then on the first Saturday evening in October we invited all our friends to a house-warming party. This was well under way when I heard shouting in the garden and went out onto the balcony to see who it was. There was Jimmy Baldwin, bleeding from a cut in his forehead, and I rushed down to help him into the living room, where everyone fell silent as he appeared. Toots took him to the bathroom to clean the blood off his face, and when they returned I asked him what had happened. He confronted me in mock fury and said he had cut his head on our gateway. 'Motherfucker!' he shouted. 'It's bad enough that you call this the Nigger House, but then you go and wrap barbed wire around your gate!' After which he smiled his brilliant toothy smile and kissed me and Toots as we helped him to the punchbowl, where he was soon surrounded by our friends, shifting the party into high gear, as he always did. Later, as everything was winding down, Jimmy and I sat out on the terrace, talking as usual of growing up poor in New York, which now seemed to both of us to be part of an irretrievably lost world.

The garden of Nigâr Hanım's house was particularly beautiful in spring, with all the flowers in full bloom and the Judas trees and wisteria vines blossoming. The last guests to leave our parties would always sit with us on the terrace around the venerable cypress tree, listening to nightingales serenading one another in the surrounding woods. After one such night the very last guest to leave was John Schereschewsky, and he and I sat out on the terrace for hours, watching a full moon soar slowly across the sky. As time passed I began to doze off and his voice seemed to grow fainter – but then I awoke, feeling distinctly warmer, to see that he had climbed up to the top of the cypress and was slowly swaying back and forth, still talking as the sun rose up out of the hills across the Bosphorus. At which point he finally climbed down and staggered home.

During the spring vacation in 1965 we went to the Greek island of Samos, crossing in a small boat from the Turkish port of Kuşadası. We had planned to spend the whole vacation there, but it was so cold and rainy we cut short our stay. We returned to Istanbul on Easter Sunday, two days earlier than planned, to discover that in our absence Mary had invited her extended family, at least a score of them, to stay in Nigâr Hanım's Köşk, and they were enjoying an Easter feast in the garden when we arrived. As soon as they saw us they scattered, gathering up their belongings and fleeing in disarray, as Mary hurriedly began cleaning up and her mother and daughter made up the beds in our rooms, where their relatives had been sleeping.

Early that evening, as I was taking a bath, Mary pounded on the bathroom door, pleading with me to come out and help her. I dressed hurriedly and went out to see what was wrong. Mary told me that Avadis and Haçik were out on the graveyard road, trying to kill one another, and she begged me to stop them. I found the two of them with bloodied heads, battering one another with rocks and cobblestones ripped up from the road. They grappled in the dust, dead drunk, both of them dressed in clothes of mine that had gone missing from our closet. I managed to separate them and told Haçik to get lost. He staggered off down the road while I led Avadis back to the house and delivered him to Mary, who gave him a tongue-lashing that drove him to bed.

For us that was the last of many straws, and the next day Toots told Mary that she and her family would have to leave, as soon as possible. Mary managed to find a job as housekeeper with an American family in Arnavutköy, the Bosphorus village where her extended family lived, and the following Saturday a hired truck came to take their things away, with the help of Avadis, Haçik and the driver.

Watching from the balcony I noticed that the last thing loaded onto the truck was a coop full of chickens. Mary had obviously been keeping them behind the house in secret – for we wouldn't have allowed them, knowing from experience that they attracted rats. As the driver started up the truck and began to drive away, Mary's cat, which had been sitting on top of their belongings, jumped off and ambled back to the köşk, seeming to know it would have a better life with us than with the Bardakcıyans.

The remote location of house led to several unlikely incidents. One evening, sitting on the balcony, I saw two men approaching along the garden path. I asked them where they were going, and one of them said they were looking for the İdeal Hotel, a high-class bordello in the woods just above the Bosphorus. So I gave them directions and they left.

I realised then that anyone could get into the house during the night, for there was no lock on the iron door leading into the ground-floor rooms where the Bardakçıyans had lived. So I contrived a makeshift burglar alarm out of empty wine and champagne bottles, piling them up inside the iron door, so that if anyone tried to open it they would come crashing down and alert me.

A few weeks later I was having my morning coffee in the kitchen when I heard someone knocking on the iron door. I removed the wall of empty bottles and opened it, to find an old shepherdess whom I had seen from time to time grazing her flock on the hillside above the fortress of Rumeli Hisarı. In her arms was a baby lamb. It had been born in our garden early that morning, she said. She had just wanted to show me the lamb, which she held tenderly as she took it back to its mother, leaving me with the feeling that I had been witness to a nativity.

The only house close to ours was the Tevfik Fikret Museum, just above us at the end of the side road that branched off from the Aşiyan road. As I later learned, the museum's two live-in custodians had formerly been guards at the sarcophagus of the famous Ottoman admiral Barbarossa, at Beşiktaş, on the Lower Bosphorus. One day a tourist had left his suitcase behind at the sarcophagus and had never returned to reclaim it. When the two of them had been reassigned to the Tevfik Fikret Museum they had brought the case along with them.

One afternoon, as Eileen was looking out of her bedroom window, she saw the two custodians fighting on the road outside. While she watched, one of them stabbed the other and then ran back towards the museum, leaving his victim lying on the ground. He must have called the local police station, for a few minutes later we heard sirens as a police car came up the side road, followed by an ambulance. The medics examined the victim and carried him to the ambulance, which then drove away. Two more police cars arrived and we saw the other custodian being taken away in one of them. The second police car parked outside our house, and a detective came in to question us. After Eileen had told him what she had seen and he had noted down her testimony, he told us what had happened. The man who had been taken away in the ambulance was dead, and the other had confessed to his murder. It seems the two had quarrelled over the suitcase they had taken from the Barbarossa sarcophagus, which led to the fatal fight. The detective said he thought it wouldn't be necessary for Eileen to testify at the trial, for the murderer would probably plead guilty in the hope of getting a reduced sentence.

But that was by no means the most unlikely incident during our time at Nigâr Hanım's Köşk. A few months later, Toots took the children to the Istanbul Zoo, where the star exhibit was Mohini the Elephant. In those days the zoo was very primitive, and none of the staff, from the director downwards, had any qualifications or experience in caring for the creatures in their charge – least of all the elephant keeper, who was a jumped-up janitor. Toots told me that when they went to see Mohini he was rocking his cage and trumpeting in what seemed to be rage and frustration as his keeper tried to feed him ground-up *simits*. The poor man looked at Toots and asked plaintively, 'What do elephants eat?'

When I heard this I called up my friend Lee Gardner, who taught zoology at Robert Academy and had worked at a zoo in the US. He went with me to the Istanbul Zoo and talked with the director and the elephant keeper, advising them on the care and feeding of Mohini.

All seems to have gone well for a couple of months, but then the zoo's director called Lee: Mohini was dead, apparently after eating poisoned food that someone had thrown into his cage. Lee offered to write to a friend of his at a zoo in India to see if they could send a replacement elephant, and he asked the director if Mohini's remains could be sent to Robert College, so that his students could study the elephant's bone structure. The director agreed. Lee could expect Mohini's remains within the week, he said.

We were having lunch in our dining room a few days later when I heard a loud knocking on the door. I went out to find a burly, unshaven workman standing there smoking a cigarette. 'We're delivering your elephant,' he said, pointing to the Aşiyan road, where on a big dump truck lay Mohini's huge carcass, with clouds of flies buzzing around it and giving off a terrible stench. I told him he had delivered it to the wrong place and, after calling Lee, I got into the truck and directed the driver up to the campus. Lee and his students were waiting for us in an open field behind his house, and I had the driver dump Mohini's remains there. Lee sprayed the carcass with a disinfectant to drive off the flies, and then he and his students began cutting the flesh away to expose the bones. I left them to their work and walked home.

In the days that followed I checked with Lee on their progress. He had sent off to a pharmaceutical firm in Germany, ordering a special type of microbe that would consume the remnants of flesh from Mohini's bones. But the microbes had been held up in Turkish customs and died. He had also arranged a replacement for Mohini from his friend's zoo in India, but the elephant too was held up in customs, where it also had died, stinking up the whole harbour before it was finally dumped deep in the Aegean.

Lee and his students worked on nonetheless, and eventually cleaned and laid out Mohini's bones so they could be studied and photographed. When they had finished, Lee called me to say they were going to bury Mohini that afternoon. Taking Brendan with me, we walked up to Lee's place, where he and his students interred the elephant's remains in a field behind the Gardners' house.

A few weeks later the spring semester ended and we went off to Naxos for the summer, after which we flew to London, where we lived for a year while I was doing postdoctoral studies at All Souls College, Oxford. By the time we returned to Istanbul Nigâr Hanım's Köşk had been requisitioned and rebuilt by the Turkish Intelligence Service. So we moved into an apartment in the Tower House, a faculty residence at the top of the Aşiyan road, where we lived until 1976 – by which time Robert College had become Bosphorus University. I left the university in June of 1976 because of the limit on foreign faculty imposed by the Turkish Ministry of Education, but I was invited back in 1993, when a new Turkish government allowed a much larger foreign faculty.

By that time the children had grown up and gone their separate ways, but then in 1995 Brendan rejoined us and began a new life in Istanbul. On the day he arrived I helped him carry his luggage to our apartment, in a valley sloping down from the main campus, just below the playground of the university nursery school. As we passed the playground Brendan said, 'The elephant's buried there.' And I realised that this was where we had watched Mohini being laid to rest twenty-nine years earlier. Ever since then, whenever I pass the elephant's grave I recall the memories of our life in Nigâr Hanım's Köşk. One more gathering place for my Istanbul ghosts.

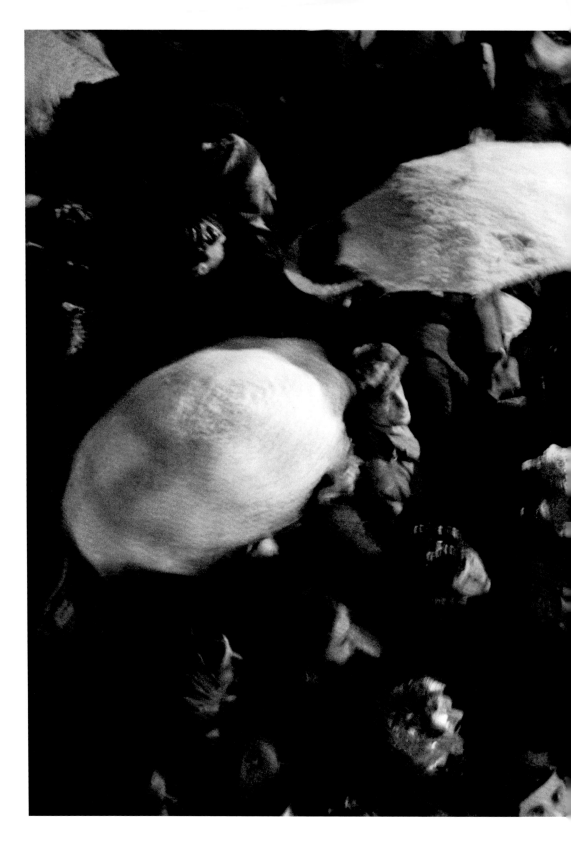

The Final Journey
By Maureen Freely

In the summer of 2015, some weeks after we laid our mother to rest in Feriköy Cemetery, alongside so many of the ghosts to whom this book is dedicated, we brought John to England, and it was here, in a little care home in Corsham in Wiltshire, that he spent the last two years of his life. His window looked out onto meadows that were green in all seasons, but most of the time he kept his curtains closed, the better to see the screen that occupied most of his waking hours. At the age of ninety he was still completing three books a year, with at least a dozen others waiting half-finished on the side. Some of these retraced his travels, others followed in the footsteps of those who had inspired those travels. One was a thriller, set in present-day Istanbul and starring a heroic anachronism named Tom, who looked and talked and acted like John, except that he was wifeless, childless and fifty years younger. Following a chance encounter with a glamorous fugitive from injustice, he goes on the run, to be aided and abetted, hidden and entertained by the twentieth-century city's greatest characters, who are, like Tom, restored to youth and perfect health.

They kept his mind agile, these exercises in remembering and imagining, as did the great piles of newspapers and periodicals he worked his way through over breakfast every morning, and the crime fiction he read at night. Despite our constant pleas to take physical exercise just as seriously, he refused to do so in our presence, preferring to tell us fantastical stories about all the miles he had travelled on the exercise bicycle we'd placed underneath his desk. If, in my capacity as bad cop, I reminded him that it did no good to lie to us, as the joke would be on him, he would smile and say nothing. But then, a few minutes later, apropos of nothing, he would say, 'I'm not afraid of death, you know. I'm just afraid of dying.'

In the meantime, he was determined to make the most of every day and moment. So, too, were the ladies who dressed, fed and bathed him, and stopped by after their rounds to listen to his stories. They took such good care of him that he was sometimes reluctant to go on outings. But, whenever he did, he found wonders wherever he looked. 'I'd forgotten how beautiful this valley was,' he'd say. 'I don't think I've ever tasted a croissant this good.' He complained about the way I navigated his wheelchair – too rough, too fast, too erratic, too reckless – and he had much too much to say about what he called his dangling participles. He sometimes admitted that he had never anticipated being this old, but never once did he complain about it.

Which was not to say he was prepared to suffer discomfort unnecessarily. He would write lists in preparation for my sister Eileen's

weekly calls from New York. Hardly a week passed without her sending him slippers, pyjamas, desks, pillows, chairs, and long-handled combs that he had perhaps exaggerated the need for. Whenever she visited, he had another list of heavy lifting jobs for her husband Tony. In exchange, he took his own social duties seriously. In preparation for book launches, birthday celebrations, Skype conversations with my brother Brendan in Istanbul, or Christmas in Manchester with his grandchildren Ariadne and Alex and the rest of the Baker clan, he would search the internet for unsuitable limericks and commit the very worst to memory.

He kept up a lively – and for the most part, more decorous – correspondence with friends on six continents – and out of these conversations came ideas for new adventures. The first, at the invitation of the Irish poet Nuala Ní Dhomhnaill, was to a literary festival in Dingle, in the West of Ireland, just a few miles away from his childhood home in Inch. Their event was in the old courthouse, which was packed, literally to the rafters, with curious locals. As it drew to a close, Nuala said, 'Well, John, you've been all around the world, and now it's time to come back to your own people.' And so, a few months later, we did. This time we went to stay in the hills above Inch Strand, in a cottage owned by a family friend whose father had been cared for by my grandmother when he was a baby.

No sooner had we arrived than his hearing aid packed up. Whereupon my daughter Helen became his scribe. She used whatever napkin or notebook was to hand to ask him large questions about his life. Towards the end of our stay, Ann Close, John's American editor, came to visit with her oncologist nephew, who was also named John. Young John would sit next to Somewhat Older John with his iPad, transcribing Ann's editorial queries by day and our dinner table conversations by night. Somewhat Older John would patiently wait for his typing to stop. Having read the latest instalment, he would gaze up at the ceiling in puzzlement, before launching into yet another elegant disquisition that was all the better for sending us in a direction that no one else at the table had anticipated.

With each return to the care home in Corsham, he seemed happier to be home. The ladies fussed over him, laughing at his every joke, even if they had heard it many times before. If they came in with his evening pills while we were watching our weekly subtitled episode of *Breaking Bad*, he would say, 'Hurry. Hurry. There's about to be another murder.' If I came to take him out for lunch, he would wave at every carer we passed on our way out, and say, 'She's taking me out for an airing.' His favourite place for entertaining the many friends who came to visit was The Methuen Arms. His favourite waiter there was a local boy named Harry Self. Every time John saw him, he would cry, 'To thine own self be free!'

The trip he spent most of his last winter planning was to New York, for the publication of his second memoir in as many years. In his first, *The Art of Exile*, he'd covered his entire life, often at a breakneck pace. In *The House of Memory*, covering just his first twenty years, he offered a more grounded account of growing up poor in New York and the West of Ireland and escaping all that by going off to war. All winter he talked about the people he wanted to see, the places he wanted to visit one last time. My sister got us business-class tickets, and when we were at last on board and settled into our seats he called my name from across the aisle and said, 'I could ride back and forth on this thing for the rest of my life.'

When we arrived later that day at our Midtown hotel, we found many more people there to greet us than we had expected. Nancy, John's sole surviving sibling, whom he had not seen in three decades, had flown in from South Carolina. Her two children – cousins I had not seen since 1963 – had flown in from Kansas. My daughter Emma flew in from Chicago with her young son Max. My daughters Helen and Pandora soon joined us from London. Over the weekend more cousins arrived, driving in with their families from New Jersey, New Hampshire and upstate New York, until there were almost thirty of us, spanning four generations.

During the week that followed, John spoke at bookstores, launch parties and on the radio. He signed mountains of books. He met his new agent, Gillian MacKenzie, to hatch new ideas. He met with the daughter of Bernard Coopersmith who, while at boot camp with my father in 1944, had reprimanded him for wishing no more from life than to be a beachcomber, and told him he should use his brain and go to college. Bernard was the first person he had ever met who had even been to college. They lost touch after boot camp, but in 1960, a week after my father was awarded his doctorate in physics, John tracked Bernard down, to tell him he had followed his advice.

Bernard's widow and his entire family had planned to come in to New York to meet him, only to be foiled by a freak blizzard. Other old friends – including the few survivors of the wild days remembered in this book – were similarly impeded. When we took John back to his old neighbourhood in Brooklyn, the drifts were still too high and the streets too icy for John to get out of the car, so we drove around from street to street, searching for landmarks that were no more. Judging from the street signs, this was now a Dominican neighbourhood. When John happened to mention that it had not been an Irish but a German neighbourhood in his day, and I asked him why they had chosen to live there, he told us what his mother had said whenever she was asked the same: 'I didn't come all the way to America to live among the Irish.' After we had passed ten streets to hear that John had once lived on seven of them, and I asked him how often they had moved, he said: 'Every time the rent was due.' As we drove through Evergreen Cemetery, where he had worked with his father in the summer during his college years, and where he had also courted our mother, John ran out of things to say, and in the photos we took of him there at the top of the hill, with his back to the panoramic view of Manhattan, he looks very sad.

The next day the sun came out, just in time for us to roll up Fifth Avenue with the Kerrymen and a police escort in the St Patrick's Day Parade. This privilege was thanks to my long-lost cousin Jeffrey, whose next-door neighbour is high up in the New York Police Department. At the tail end of the parade was a reception at the American Irish Historical Society, just across the street from the Metropolitan Museum. They took John up to the party in a tiny, creaky lift that had not seen a human being in many decades. We were just preparing to leave an hour or so later when we were joined by fifty or more Roses of Tralee and elsewhere, who sang and danced for us before vanishing in the blink of an eye.

From there it was more friends, more former students, and another giant reunion, this time with my mother's family. Business Class, when we finally returned to it, was eerily, but also soothingly, quiet. But

no sooner had we reached Corsham than John turned to me to say, 'Next stop Greece.'

He spent much of the next month trying to convince me that there could not be a better place than Naxos, an island of mountains, cliffs and stairs, for a man in a wheelchair. The matter was yet to be settled when the care home rang me to say that John had been rushed into hospital in the middle of the night, having fallen while running a high fever.

He had fractured his spine, but what took him was a vicious infection that they finally traced to the lining of his heart. He seemed to be rallying, but on his eighth night in hospital he went into a decline. The next day he informed me that he was ready to go, so could I please organise the execution.

When I told him that was not how things were done in England, he rolled his eyes, the same way he'd done when I was a child and taking my time to get up and help my mother set the table. The next thing he said was, 'Take me to Toots.' He would not rest until I had promised.

Like his mother and grandfather before him, my father was a devout Catholic atheist. But by the time he was writing the book in your hand, he had become intrigued, even obsessed, with myths that promised some form of eternal life. There was the River of Paradise, somewhere near Tibet. There were the Celtic legends, still marking the stones of the wild peninsula of his childhood. But most of all, there were his Stamboul Ghosts, whom he now placed in Homer's Land of Dreams. On his last day he seemed to be preparing to join them – not to rest, but to set out on what he was suddenly calling a peregrination.

There were things he needed to do before he left. One was to discover where words come from. He was going into a panic, knowing that time might run out before he had the final answer. So I reminded him that my son Matthew, who has a doctorate in evolutionary linguistics and cognition, was perhaps uniquely qualified to take on the task. By some miracle, we were able to reach him by Skype in Australia. Having handed over, John was at last able to lie back on his pillow, to prepare for the final journey.

This turned out to be as riddled with reversals and surprises as the journeys he took in life. There was, in the first instance, the avalanche of grief – for somehow we had all

expected him to be with us for so much longer. We heard not just his friends from six continents, and hundreds of former students, but also our own childhood friends, including Magali's son, Larry Morgan, who now runs a safari park in South Africa. They all wanted to know about the funeral. Most expected it to happen quickly, having had no experience of the British way of death, which involves the doctor's report going to a pathologist in another city, and then going back to the doctor for clarification, before being sent back to the pathologist, who, when he gets back from annual leave, passes it on to the coroner, who sends it back to the hospital, which then contacts the family, inviting them to make an appointment with the registrar sometime during the following week. Only when the family has possession of the death certificate can the funeral director contact the crematorium to make a booking.

The delays made no sense to our Turkish friends, who are accustomed to funerals happening almost overnight. But for us there was also the matter of Feriköy Cemetery, which is managed by the European consulates on a rotation basis. This was the year of the Dutch. After a flurry of electronic misdirection, we found an old friend who was friends with the consul's wife.

Once the burial of the ashes had been approved, we needed to arrange for a hole to be dug in the double plot where our mother was already resting. This time it was my old classmate Tony Greenwood who saved the day. He was able to direct Aslan Bey, who looks after the cemetery, to the correct location after it emerged that he was intending to bury my father with Tony's mother.

Tony also helped us arrange the memorial service at the university, as well the opening of the building the university has named after him – just a few paces away from the burial place of that elephant. It was just after the burial at Feriköy, that Aslan Bey suggested we might commission a graveside fountain in our father's name, so that he and all his Ghosts might be more easily and regularly watered. And once we children had agreed to this excellent idea, we decided we would pay for it with the proceeds of this book.

Soon there was only one snag left, and that was the question of taking John's ashes back to Turkey. It seemed to be illegal to take foreign ashes into the country, though no one was completely sure, and no one in the Turkish consulate was given to answering a phone. In the end, the shipbuilder son of a family friend valiantly offered to meet us in the baggage hall with his customs agent, to help in the event of a problem. We were just boarding the plane when he texted to say that he had been called away on business. He advised us simply to go through Nothing to Declare, looking as if we didn't. Everything would be fine, he assured us. His chauffeur would be waiting on the other side. And so he was.

The next day we took John's ashes in their tiny casket to Feriköy Cemetery, where Father Ian Sherwood gave him an Anglican burial that was as beautiful and moving as the service his fictitious alter ego performed in my father's thriller.

We left John next to my mother, and just a few paces away from Keith and Joanne Greenwood, David and Ann Garwood, and Hilary Sumner-Boyd, who were all at that party you just read about, when the punch bowl broke to send its contents pouring down the cobblestone road below. In these pages he said that the punch bowl had been filled with vodka. I know from other bearers of that legend that it was most certainly

eggnog, which was why all those
thirsty pets converging out of nowhere
were able to find it and lap it up,
as the Greenwoods and Garwoods
and Boyds hid in the shadows, praying
that their clean-living neighbours
hadn't noticed.

Now here they all were, together
again. As we stood before our parents'
headstone, I could almost hear them
conferring in elated whispers. Even
after we had moved on, to finish the
evening at Asmalı Cavit – John's
favourite restaurant – I could almost
see them, setting off on their
peregrination, in the Land of Dreams.

John Freely's favourite Beyoğlu meyhane, Asmalı Cavit, by Monica Fritz, 2018

AYÇA OĞUŞ

Ara Güler and His Photographs

The beautiful images that adorn this memoir are by the great Ara Güler (above in 2015). His work as a photojournalist for Magnum took him all over the world, and his archive of eight hundred thousand negatives contains likenesses of Salvador Dalí, Marc Chagall, Ansel Adams, Alfred Hitchcock, Willy Brandt, John Berger, Maria Callas, Bertrand Russell, Pablo Picasso, Indira Gandhi and Winston Churchill, amongst others. But it is his chronicling of mid-twentieth-century Istanbul for which he is most loved.

At a time when anyone who could was fleeing to the new suburbs, Ara chose to remain in the heart of the old European city, bringing up his family and situating his office in the apartments overlooking İstiklâl and Galatasaray, above what had once been his father's pharmacy. The beer halls so beloved by my father were just a few paces away. Here, over the years, there grew between them the sort of deep and unshakeable affection that can only exist between men who share no language. Once, during one of Turkey's more nervous political moments, Ara walked into the Pasaj to see my father perched on his favourite stool. He opened

his arms wide as he rushed towards him, only to find himself pinned to the ground by my father's favourite bartender, who had mistaken Ara for a dangerous revolutionary. There followed hours of laughter, bear hugs, mortified apologies, and *Arjantins* on the house.

Ara is Armenian, and as proud to be Armenian as he is proud to be a Turk. But his camera knows no nationality or religion. Wherever he points it there are layers and layers of history, but what draws his eye is the human figure passing through it all, reaching for an umbrella, a cigarette, a fish. Even when he is in a gallery packed with crowds admiring his art, he refuses to call himself an artist. He does not, I think, enjoy being the object of admiration. He prefers to blend into the background, as when I last saw him, sitting by the wall in the little café they opened up on the ground floor of his building some years ago and named after him. On the walls around him were reproductions of his most famous photographs. Close at hand was a devoted waiter, watching over him while he witnessed life unfolding, everywhere he looked.

Maureen Freely

Cover
A street in Tarlabaşı,
Beyoğlu, 1965

Back cover and page 24
A fisherman's café in
Sarıyer, on the Upper
Bosphorus, 1982

Pages 4–5
Cicim Sokak in the Tomtom
district of Beyoğlu, the
old European quarter

Pages 6–7
Drink and music in
Beyoğlu, 1969

Pages 18–19
Rush hour in the snow
on the Galata Bridge,
1958 (detail of p106)

Page 20
A snowy day in the
Old City district of
Küçük Ayasofya, 1968

Page 22–23
A Bosphorus ferry
sets off at nightfall from
the village of Kandilli

Page 30–31
A bar in the
dockland district of
Tophane, 1959

Page 32
The artist Aliye
Berger-Boronai in 1957

Page 44–45
Büyükada, or
Prinkipo, largest of
the Princes Islands

Page 46
Commuters board
the 'Küçüksu' ferry in
Beylerbeyi, 1965

Pages 70–71
The busy shopping
street of İstiklâl
Caddesi, 1992

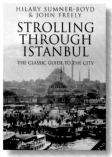

Page72
*Strolling Through
Istanbul*, first
published in 1972

Page 36–37
Aliye Berger-Boronai in
her studio in the Narmanlı
Yurdu, Beyoğlu, 1971

Page 40–41
Aliye, 'Queen of Pera',
1971. Her soirées
were legendary

Page 54
Customers dancing
in a 'music saloon',
Beyoğlu, 1969

Pages 60–61
Barges and birds
on the Golden
Horn, 1956

Page 62
The cruise liner
'Olympia' seen from
the Galata Bridge, 1959

Pages 80–81
Balıkpazarı, the
Beyoğlu fish market

Page 82
A Beyoğlu
meyhane, 1954

Pages 92–93
Metin Eloğlu, painter
and poet, at his *köşk*
in Erenköy, 1957

Page 94
Dozing off at a
coffee house in
Paşabahçe, 1951

Page 115
Fruit for sale in the old
Stamboul quarter of
Zeyrek, 1959

Page 116–117
A coffee house in
Anadoluhisarı, on the
Asian shore, 1994

Page 104–105
The ferry at Kandilli
on a winter's
evening, 1965

Page 106
The Yeni Cami seen
from the Galata
Bridge, 1958

Pages 126–127
Fedoras and
umbrellas,
winter 1963

Page 128
Island ferries
docking at the
Galata Bridge, 1955.

A Cornucopia Book

Published in 2018 by
Caique Publishing Ltd,
1 Rutland Court,
Edinburgh EH3 8AY,
in association with
Kayık Yayıncılık Ltd,
Valikonağı Caddesi 64,
Nişantaşı, 34367 Istanbul

ISBN 978-0-9565948-8-4
ISBN 978-605-83080-4-6

PROJECT EDITORS
John Scott, Berrin Torolsan

DESIGN Clive Crook

TEXT EDITORS
Hilary Stafford-Clark
Susana Raby

Printed and bound in Turkey
by Ofset Yapımevi, Istanbul
www.ofset.com

CORNUCOPIA BOOKS
PO Box 13311,
Hawick TD9 7YF, Scotland
www.cornucopia.net

With special thanks to
the Ara Güler Archives
and Research Centre,
and the Ara Güler Museum,
Istanbul (Ara Güler Arşiv
ve Araştırma Merkezi,
ve Ara Güler Müzesi)

The portrait of Hayalet Oğuz
by Gürdal Duyar, page 79,
is from O Pera'daki Hayalet,
by Sezer Duru and Orhan
Duru (5th edition, YKY,
Istanbul, June 2018)